ACCLAIM

DALLAS MORNING NEWS

While the process of forgiveness may seem Herculean to the person who holds grudges, Arnold leaves one feeling that if the remarkable people in these stories can forgive, anyone can.

NATIONAL EXAMINER

Gut-wrenching, real-life sagas...

PUBLISHERS WEEKLY

Noteworthy for its profound and always timely subject matter, this book includes story after story of people who have forgiven despite unfathomable personal tragedy and a vengeful cultural climate...Not one to engage in long theological explorations, Arnold instead allows many of his subjects to speak for themselves...In all cases, he reminds us that to forgive is neither to excuse nor to anesthetize ourselves from the pain that attends life and love, but rather to enter again into life's fray.

DENVER POST

Why Forgive? shows humanity at its gut-churning worst and ennobling best through the experience of people who have endured unthinkable losses and struggled to make peace with their perpetrators.

Why Forgive?

JOHANN CHRISTOPH ARNOLD

ORBIS BOOKS
Maryknoll, New York 10545

Founded in 1970, Orbis Books endeavors to publish works that enlighten the mind, nourish the spirit, and challenge the conscience. The publishing arm of the Maryknoll Fathers and Brothers, Orbis seeks to explore the global dimensions of the Christian faith and mission, to invite dialogue with diverse cultures and religious traditions, and to serve the cause of reconciliation and peace. The books published reflect the views of their authors and do not represent the official position of the Maryknoll Society. To learn more about Maryknoll and Orbis Books, please visit our website at www.maryknoll.org.

Copyright © 2000 by The Plough Publishing House of The Bruderhof Foundation, Inc., Farmington PA 15437.

Originally published by The Plough Publishing House of The Bruderhof Foundation, Inc. *Why Forgive?* is a revised and expanded version of Arnold's book *Seventy Times Seven* (1997).

This edition published in 2003 by Orbis Books, Maryknoll, NY 10545-0308.
All rights reserved.

Manufactured in the United States of America
ISBN 1-57075-512-4

The Library of Congress has catalogued the original edition as follows:

Library of Congress Cataloging-in-Publcation Data

Arnold, Johann Christoph, 1940-
    Why forgive? / Johann Christoph Arnold.
        p. cm.
Rev. ed. of: Seventy Times Seven. Includes index
    ISBN: 0-87486-992-7 (alk. paper)
    1.Forgiveness—Religious aspects—Bruderhof Communities. I. Arnold, Johann
    Christoph, 1940-Sevemtu times seven. II. Title.
        BV4647.F55 A76 2000
        234'.5—dc21

                                                            99-050827
                                                            CIP

There is a hard law…

When an injury is done to us,

we never recover until we forgive.

ALAN PATON

To: Chantal mighty

From: Johann Christoph Arnold . . . .

CONTENTS

FOREWORD

What do you do when your friend gives you a sawed-off shotgun? For Roger, this was an easy question to answer. He used it. And he says that if he had the chance, he'd use it again. Roger's entire life has become consumed by one unquenchable desire: avenging his daughter's death.

Sarah was out on her bike when she was hit by drunk driver. She died almost instantly. There was no doubt about who was to blame, and the driver (who didn't have a valid license because of a previous drunk driving conviction) was sent to prison for manslaughter. But that wasn't enough for Roger. He borrowed a gun and – when the driver was released from prison – shot him, fully intending to kill him.

So now the tables were turned, and Roger found himself charged with attempted murder and faced with the possibility of a long prison sentence. Astonishingly, he was found "not guilty." Despite the fact that he had deliberately tried to take a man's life, the jury found his victim – who had never once shown the slightest remorse – so repulsive that they unanimously acquitted Roger. Even so, he wasn't satisfied: if anything, he was more determined than ever to avenge his daughter's death. I asked him if squeezing a trigger and watching a man collapse in agony made him feel any better. "No," he said. "Only killing him could make me feel better." I asked his wife, Cathy, how she felt. Her answer was even more chilling. "I could never be happy if Roger killed him," she told me, "because that would mean that I hadn't killed him. I need to pull that trigger myself. I need to see him dead, and know I'm responsible."

Sitting with them in their house, I was overwhelmed by their anger and pain, and by the horror of their ordeal. There was little doubt in my mind that justice had not been served by the light punishment given their daughter's killer: his self-centered callousness shocked me to the core. Yet I also couldn't help feeling that their continued bitterness over her death was compounding their misery.

Having been through one hell, it seemed to me that their inability to forgive and let go was putting them through another. Day after day they were letting new hatred and resentment consume them. Was this really what their daughter would have wanted for them – this living hell that was destroying their lives, but which had no impact on that of her killer?

Is there any way that people like Roger and Cathy can learn to forgive? Can they ever be released from the anger that tortures them? In *Why Forgive?* Johann Christoph Arnold tries to answer these questions. The book is full of stories of people who, often against great odds, found strength to forgive those who wronged them, and in doing so found peace: people like Bud Welch, whose daughter was killed in the Oklahoma City bombing, or Phan Thi Kim Phuc, whose photograph as a napalm-burned, naked nine-year-old running for her life became one of the Vietnam War's most recognizable images. It also contains stories that take place closer to home – the business partner locked in a bitter quarrel, the wife reeling from the discovery that her husband has cheated on her, the victim of childhood abuse.

Arnold retells the stories gathered here with compassion and without judgment. They are moving and compelling, and no one who reads them will be quite the same again. They challenge us to explore a side of our nature that, if unchecked, threatens to devour us. More important, they offer a way out of bitterness, toward forgiveness and reconciliation. But don't take my word for it. Read them for yourself.

Steve Chalke

PROLOGUE

One morning in September 1995, as I sat drinking coffee and reading the paper, I was horrified to see headlines reporting the abduction, in broad daylight, of a local seven-year-old girl. Within a week the primary suspect – a trusted acquaintance of the child's family – confessed to the crime. After luring her into in a wooded area near her home, he had raped her, beaten her to death, and hidden her.

The public's reaction was predictable: this man deserved to die. Under the state's new capital punishment statute, he was regarded as a prime candidate. Initially the District Attorney promised to seek a maximum of twenty years in exchange for information leading to the recovery of the girl's body, but he went back on his word after it was found, saying he would have made a pact with the devil to find the child. He also said that he hoped to become the first DA in recent New York history to send a murderer to the death chamber. Residents interviewed by the local news media even suggested that the authorities release him so they could "take care of him."

While this rage was understandable, I wondered how it could possibly bring solace to the victim's grieving family. As a pastor, I felt fairly certain what my response should be: I arranged for someone from my congregation to go to the funeral, and I sent flowers to the child's parents. I tried (unsuccessfully) to visit the family. But my heart was still heavy. Somehow, I felt I had to visit the murderer – at this point still a faceless monster – and confront him with the horror of his actions. I wanted to help him see that if he was ever going to find peace with himself after committing such a heinous crime, it could only be through lifelong remorse.

I knew people would look askance at such a visit, if not entirely misinterpret it, but I was convinced it was my duty. So it was that a few months later I found myself sitting alone in the county jail, face to face with the uncuffed killer. The hours I spent in that cell shook me deeply and left many unresolved questions – questions, in fact, that eventually led me to write this book.

Less than three months after my visit, the murderer faced his victim's family in court. The room was packed, and entering it, one could feel a wave of hostility. First the sentence – life imprisonment without parole – was read out, and then the judge added: "I hope that the hell you now face in prison is only a foretaste of the hell you will face in eternity."

The defendant was then allowed a few words. In a loud, wavering voice, he told the girl's parents that he was "truly sorry" for the pain he had caused – and that he was praying daily for forgiveness. As a ripple of angry whispers spread through the audience, I asked myself, How can such a man ever be forgiven?

1

The Cancer of Bitterness

Whoever opts for revenge should dig two graves.

CHINESE PROVERB

Forgiveness is a door to peace and happiness. It is a small, narrow door, and cannot be entered without stooping. It is also hard to find. But no matter how long the search, it *can* be found. At least that is what the men and women in this book have discovered. By reading their stories, perhaps you, too, will be led to the door of forgiveness. Just remember that once there, only you can open it.

What does forgiving really mean? Clearly it has little to do with human fairness, which demands an eye for an eye, or with excusing, which means brushing something aside. Life is never fair, and it is full of things that can never be excused.

When we forgive someone for a mistake or a deliberate hurt, we still recognize it as such, but instead of lashing out or biting back, we attempt to see beyond it, so as to restore our relationship with the person responsible for it. Our forgiveness may not take away our pain – it may not even be acknowledged or accepted – yet the act of offering it will keep us from being sucked into the downward spiral of resentment. It will also guard us against the temptation of taking out our anger or hurt on someone else.

It is only natural, when we are hurt, to want to revisit the source of that hurt. There is nothing wrong with that. Whenever we do this in the sense of chalking up another person's guilt, however, our pain will soon turn into resentment. It doesn't matter if the cause of our pain is real or imagined: the effect is the same. Once there, it will slowly eat away at us until it spills out and corrodes everything around us.

We all know bitter people. They have an amazing memory for the tiniest detail, and they wallow in self-pity and resentment. They catalog every offense and are always ready to show others how much they have been hurt. On the outside they may appear to be calm and composed, but inside they are about to burst with pent-up feelings.

Bitter people defend their grudges constantly: they feel that they have been hurt too deeply and too often, and that this exempts them from the need to forgive. But it is just these people who need to forgive most of all. Their hearts are sometimes so full of rancor that they no longer have the capacity to love.

Almost twenty years ago my father and I were asked by a colleague to visit an acquaintance who claimed she could no longer love. Jane's husband lay dying, and she longed to comfort him, yet something seemed to hold her back from within. Jane was by all accounts a blameless person: she was neat, meticulous, capable, hard-working, and honest – yet in talking with her it became clear that she was as unfeeling as a rock. She really could not love.

After months of counseling, the cause of Jane's coldness finally became clear: she was unable to forgive. She couldn't point to a single large hurt, but emotionally she was tied down – in fact, almost completely incapacitated – by the collective weight of a thousand small grudges.

Thankfully Jane was later able to overcome herself and rediscover the joy of living. That was not the case with Brenda, another embittered woman I attempted to counsel. Sexually abused by her uncle for years and silenced by her alcoholism, which her tormentor supported with daily gifts of vodka, she had finally escaped from him, but she was still under his thrall.

When I met Brenda she had been offered intensive psychiatric counseling. She also had a good job and an extensive network of supportive friends, who had made every effort to get her back on her feet. In spite of this she seemed to make no progress. Her emotions swung widely, from excited laughter to inconsolable weeping. She binged on food one day and fasted and purged the next. And she drank – bottle after bottle.

Brenda was without question the innocent victim of a horribly depraved man, yet the better I got to know her the more it seemed that she was perpetuating her own misery. In refusing to lay aside her hatred for her uncle, she was continuing to let him exert his influence over her.

Brenda was one of the most difficult people I have ever tried to help. Again and again I tried to get her to see that until she could forgive her uncle – or at least see beyond the fact that he had abused her – she would in effect remain his victim. But my efforts were in vain. Increasingly angry and confused, she drove herself deeper and deeper into a jungle of despair. Finally she attempted to strangle herself and had to be hospitalized.

The wounds left by sexual abuse take years to heal; often they leave permanent scars. Yet they need not result in life-long torment or in suicide. For every case like Brenda's, I know of others where the victims have found freedom and a new lease on life by forgiving.

Forgiving does not mean forgetting or condoning a wrong. Certainly it does not depend on a face-to-face meeting with the person responsible for it, which – in the case of sexual abuse, at least – may not even be advisable. But it does mean making a conscious decision to stop hating, because hating can never help.

Bitterness is more than a negative outlook on life. It is a destructive and self-destructive power. Like a dangerous mold or spore, it thrives in the dark recesses of the heart and feeds on every new thought of spite or hatred that comes our way. And like an ulcer aggravated by worry or a heart condition made worse by stress, it can be physically as well as emotionally debilitating.

Anne Coleman, a Delaware woman I met at a conference several years ago, experienced this firsthand:

> One day in 1985 I picked up the phone to hear my niece in Los Angeles say, "Anne, Frances has been shot. She's dead."
>
> I can't remember screaming, but I did. I made plans to fly out to California immediately, and on the plane I really thought I could kill someone. If I'd had a weapon and the murderer, I probably would have done just that.
>
> By the time I got off the plane I was getting concerned about how I was going to greet my son Daniel, who was flying in from Hawaii. Daniel was an army sergeant, and he had been trained to kill.
>
> When we got to the police station the next morning, the only thing they told us was that my daughter was

dead, and that everything else was none of our business. Sadly, this remained the case throughout the days we stayed in Los Angeles. The violent crimes coordinator told me that if they hadn't arrested someone in four days, I shouldn't expect an arrest: "We just have too many homicides in this precinct – we spend only four days on homicides."

This enraged my son Daniel. When he found out that the police department was really not interested in finding his sister's killer, he said he was going to go out and buy an Uzi and mow people down.

They hadn't really prepared us for what we would see when we picked up her car from the pound. Frances had bled to death in her car. The bullets had passed through her aorta, her heart, both lungs. She had choked on her own blood. She died early on a Sunday morning, and we picked up the car late Tuesday afternoon. It stank. That smell never left Daniel's mind, and he wanted vengeance in the worst way. He really wanted someone to do something – some kind of justice for his sister.

Over the next two-and-a-half years I saw Daniel go downhill, and then I stood alongside his sister's grave to watch him being lowered into the ground. He had finally taken revenge – on himself. I saw what hatred does: it takes the ultimate toll on one's mind and body.

Believe in Miracles

Hope for a great sea-change
On the far side of revenge.
Believe that a further shore
Is reachable from here.
Believe in miracles
And cures and healing wells.

SEAMUS HEANEY

Gordon Wilson held his daughter's hand as they lay trapped beneath a mountain of rubble. It was 1987, and he and Marie had been attending a peaceful memorial service in Enniskillen, Northern Ireland, when a terrorist bomb went off. By the end of the day Marie and nine other civilians were dead, and sixty-three had been hospitalized for injuries.

Amazingly Gordon refused to retaliate, saying that angry words could neither restore his daughter nor bring peace to Belfast. Only hours after the bombing, he told BBC reporters:

> I have lost my daughter, and we shall miss her. But I bear no ill will. I bear no grudge…That will not bring her back…Don't ask me, please, for a purpose…I don't have an answer. But I know there has to be a plan. If I didn't think that, I would commit suicide. It's part of a greater plan…and we shall meet again.

Later Gordon said that his words were not intended as a theological response to his daughter's murder. He had simply blurted them out from the depth of his heart. In the days and weeks that followed the bombing, he struggled to live up to his words. It wasn't easy, but they were something to hang on to, something to keep him afloat in the dark hours when grief overwhelmed him.

He knew that the terrorists who took his daughter's life were anything but remorseful, and he maintained that they should be punished and imprisoned. Even so, he refused to seek revenge.

> Those who have to account for this deed will have to face a judgement of God, which is way beyond my forgiveness…It would be wrong for me to give any impression that gunmen and bombers should be allowed to walk the streets freely. But…whether or not they are judged here on earth by a court of law…I do my very

best in human terms to show forgiveness...The last word rests with God.

Gordon was misunderstood and ridiculed by many because of his stand, but he says that without having made a decision to forgive, he never could have accepted the fact that his daughter was never coming back. Nor could he have found the freedom to move on. Forgiving also had a positive effect that reached beyond his personal life. At least temporarily, his words broke the cycle of killing and revenge: the local Protestant paramilitary leadership felt so convicted by his courage that they did not retaliate.

If Gordon's ability to forgive as quickly as he did seems admirable, it is also unusual. For most of us – as for Piri Thomas, a man readers may know for his autobiography, *Down These Mean Streets* – forgiveness does not come so easily:

> Whenever I hear the phrase "forgive and forget," my thoughts flow back to the forties and fifties, to the ghettoes of New York. There, where violence was and still is a part of life, so many times I heard people who had been wronged refuse when they were asked for forgiveness. Or, they would compromise with "OK, OK, I'll forgive you, but I sure won't forget."

I have been among the countless who have made that same angry promise. I remember the painful trauma I suffered when my mother Dolores passed away. She was thirty-four, I was seventeen. I got very angry at God for not letting my mother live, and refused to forgive God for being so inconsiderate. As time went by, I forgave God, but for a very long time I couldn't forget because of the great pain alive in my heart.

At the age of twenty-two, I became involved in a series of armed robberies with three other men. In the commission of the last armed robbery, there was a shoot-out with the police. I was shot by one of the officers, whom I shot in return. The policeman recovered. Otherwise I would not be writing this article, for I would have been put to death in the electric chair at Sing Sing.

While I was recovering in the prison ward of Bellevue Hospital, one of the three gunmen, a man named Angelo, turned state's evidence against me. Angelo was like a brother to me. We had both grown up on the same block of 104th Street. Angelo ratted on me about some past unarmed robberies because detectives at the 23rd Precinct threatened to beat him up so badly that even his own mother would not be able to recognize him. Angelo held up for as long as he could and then spilled out to the detectives what was and never was. When I was released from Bellevue Hospital, I was incarcerated in the Manhattan Tombs to await trial, where I found out that all that Angelo had confessed to had been dumped on me...

To make a long story short, I was sentenced to five to ten and five to fifteen years to run concurrently, at hard labor, first at Sing Sing and then at Comstock.

From time to time over the years, I would steam with anger over Angelo's betrayal, which had led to two armed robbery warrants hanging over me in the South Bronx. In my cell at night I would find myself fantasizing on ways to kill him or at least hurt him so bad he would beg for death. Angelo and I had been tight brothers from the streets. I loved him as such, but now in prison I hated him and only wanted to get even with him in the worst way. To tell the truth, I fought against these murderous feelings over the years and even prayed to get those violent thoughts out of my mind. Sometimes for long periods of time, I would forget all about Angelo, but when least expected, thought of his betrayal would pop up inside of me.

I was finally released in 1957 and was ordered to report to both a parole officer and a probation officer each week. Back out in the streets, I couldn't help thinking what would happen if I ran into Angelo. I never went looking for him because I really didn't want to find him.

I was attending a small church on 118th Street, utilizing it as a half-way house to keep me free from the gravity of those mean streets. I would think about Angelo from time to time and feel the anger still alive in my heart. I never met up with him and found better things to occupy my mind, like working on the book I started in prison, meeting a young woman named Nelin, and feeling the joy of falling in love with Nelin and sharing the same warm feelings. Angelo began to diminish and slowly fade away from my mind.

One balmy summer evening we were walking on Third Avenue. Nelin and I were happily checking out jewelry stores, pricing engagement and wedding rings. As we left one jewelry store for another, I heard someone softly call out my name: "*Oye,* Piri." I knew without a doubt that the voice belonged to Angelo. I turned to look. His once young face now showed deep lines of stress, caused perhaps by having to look so often over his shoulder. I felt the rumbling of some long ago anger trying to rise like bile out of my guts. I suppressed the urge and waited patiently to listen to whatever Angelo had to say.

Nelin pulled at my arm to get my attention and then asked me with her eyes if this was the man I had mentioned with so much anger. She whispered, *"Por favor,* Piri, don't forget what we have talked about."

I nodded and turned back to Angelo, who swallowed hard, not so much out of fear but rather as if he badly needed to get something out that he had been waiting to say for a very long time. His voice was soft.

"Piri, I have hurt everybody I loved, and that sure includes you. In the police station they began to beat me so bad, I couldn't take it. Could you please forgive me for ratting, bro?"

I stared at him, wondering how he could have the nerve to be calling me bro after ratting on me, but at the same time happy to be called bro by him once again.

"I will understand if you don't, but it took this long for me to build up my nerve. And even if you don't, I still had to try, so *por favor,* what do you say, Piri?"

I stared at Angelo and only answered when I felt Nelin squeeze my hand. The words that came from my heart lifted a great weight from my soul, and I felt my spirit soar free.

"Sure bro, I forgive you. They say everybody's got a breaking point, and that includes me. So on God's truth, Angelo, I not only forgive you, bro, it's also forgotten and to that I swear on Mom's grave."

The tears that exploded from Angelo's eyes matched my own.

"Gracias, Piri, for years I've hated my guts for not having the heart to keep from ratting on you. If I could live that all over again, I would let them beat me to death rather than turn on you. *Gracias,* bro, for your forgiving and forgetting, and I mean that from my heart."

Angelo put his hand out and then started to draw it back, as if not wanting to push his luck. My right hand reached out quickly and shook his hand with great sincerity and felt Angelo squeeze my own. We hugged briefly, and then with a smile he nodded to me and Nelin, and said "See you around, bro" and then walked away. I put my arm around Nelin's shoulders, she slipped her arm around my waist, and we both watched Angelo as he disappeared around the corner. I couldn't help thinking about something Nelin once told me she had read: "To err is human, to forgive divine."

It sure is hard to forgive, but as my father Juan often said, "Everything is hard until you learn it, and then it becomes easy." I had learned. I had not only forgiven my street brother Angelo, but I had also learned to forgive myself for having carried a thirst for revenge for so many years. I felt like the morning sunrise was coming up in my heart. I took Nelin's hand in my own and with smiles we headed towards the next jewelry store. Love in me was at last free from the weight of hate.

I never saw my bro Angelo again, for he moved to another city, and it was with sorrow that I learned some years later that he had been murdered because of money he owed a loan shark.

But I will always be glad that I forgave Angelo. I have learned that the cruelest prison of all is the prison of an unforgiving mind and spirit.

Sometimes, even when we recognize the need to forgive, we are tempted to claim that we cannot. It is simply too hard, too difficult – something for saints, maybe, but not the rest of us. We have been hurt just one time too many, we think, or misunderstood. Our side of the story has not been adequately heard.

To me, the amazing thing about Gordon and Piri's stories is that they did not weigh their options, but decided to forgive on the spur of a moment, and did so from the bottom of their hearts. If they hadn't, they might never have been able to forgive at all.

Ending the Cycle of Hatred

If only there were evil people somewhere insidiously
committing evil deeds, and it were necessary only to
separate them from the rest of us and destroy them! But
the line dividing good and evil cuts through the heart of
every human being. And who is willing to destroy a piece
of his own heart?

ALEKSANDR SOLZHENITSYN

Recited by millions from childhood on, the Lord's Prayer
includes the plea, "Forgive us our debts, as we forgive our
debtors." Familiar as it is, I often wonder whether we really
mean what we say when we repeat these words, and
whether we sufficiently consider their meaning. To me, at
least, they imply that once we recognize our own need for
forgiveness, we will be able to forgive. This recognition
does not come to most of us easily, because it demands
humility. But isn't humility the essence of forgiveness?

In the Beatitudes, Jesus tells us that the meek will be
blessed and inherit the earth. And in the parable of the
unmerciful servant, he warns us not to treat others any
more harshly than we would want to be treated:

> A rich man wanted to settle accounts with his servants.
> One of them, who owed him several thousand pounds,
> was brought in front of him, unable to pay. Because he
> was defaulting on the loan, the rich man ordered that
> the servant should be sold into slavery, together with his
> wife and children, to repay the debt. Although the rich
> man was within his legal rights to demand this, the ser-
> vant begged him for patience. So the rich man took pity
> on him. He cancelled the debt and let him go. But the
> experience left the servant badly shaken, worried about
> the state of his finances, and no sooner had he returned
> home than he went to a friend, who still owed him a
> small amount of money, and demanded repayment. His
> friend was also unable to pay, and begged the servant for
> mercy, but he refused. Instead, he had his friend thrown
> into prison.
>
> When the other servants saw what he had done, they
> were very upset and told the rich man everything. The
> rich man was furious, and called him in to answer for
> his actions: "You begged me to cancel your debt, so I did.
> Why didn't you show the same level of mercy to your
> friend as I showed to you?" In his anger, the rich man
> turned him over to the jailers to be tortured, until he
> could pay back all he owed.

In my experience, the strongest motivation for forgiveness is always the sense of having received forgiveness ourselves, or – if we do not have that – an awareness that, like everyone else in the human race, we are imperfect and have done things we need to be forgiven for.

Jared, an African-American student from Boston, says that was definitely the case with him:

> I was six years old when I awoke to the reality of racism: from the sheltered environment of my home, I was pushed out into the world – a local elementary school just down the road from our house. I went there for only a month before city law mandated that I be bussed across town to another school. My parents were not happy with this; they wanted me to go to a school where I was known and loved. They owned a farm out in the country, and so we moved there...
>
> My father, a veteran of the civil rights movement, taught me love and respect for everyone – white or black. They tried to teach me not to see everything in life along racial lines. All the same, I was the only black child in my new school, and many of the other children had obviously been taught to hate.
>
> Children can be brutal about each other's differences. They may begin with an innocent question – "Why is your skin brown?" – but then they start to laugh at you and mock you, because somewhere along the line they have been taught that if you're different – not "normal" – there's something wrong with you.

I was a fish out of water, and these kids didn't make it easy for me. I'll never forget one especially painful incident: I introduced one of my white friends to another white kid on the bus one day, and from then on they always sat together but left me out.

Later I moved to a different school, and by the time I was in the seventh grade, the tables had turned completely. Our class was now all black, except for one white guy in my class, Shawn, who was the only white in the whole school. We treated him as an outcast and taunted him with racial epithets and physically abused him. We took out our hatred of white people on him even though he hadn't done anything to harm any of us. We were angry.

Shawn symbolized everything that we knew about whites and their history: the humiliation of our people, the lynchings, the mobs, and the slave trade. We took out all our bitterness and anger on him.

I was never able to apologize to Shawn. By the time I saw my racism for what it was, we had parted ways. But I did ask God to forgive me for the harm I caused Shawn, and I resolved to forgive the guys who didn't have a heart for me when I was the only black kid in their midst.

Hela Ehrlich, a Jewish friend, has a similar story. Hela grew up in Nazi Germany, and though her immediate family escaped the death camps by emigrating just before the outbreak of World War II, her grandparents on both sides and all her childhood friends lost their lives in the Holocaust.

For many people, the passage of time softens heartache; for Hela, the opposite occurred. Slowly, almost imperceptibly, her hurt turned into bitterness, and her pain into anger. Hela did not want to be bitter; she wanted to be free to live and love. In fact, she struggled constantly to keep from hardening her heart. But she could not forgive.

Then one day it dawned on her: she would never be able to forgive her family's executioners until she was able to see that despite their guilt, they were still fellow human beings.

> Trembling, I realized that if I looked into my own heart I could find seeds of hatred there, too. Arrogant thoughts, feelings of irritation toward others, coldness, anger, envy, and indifference – these are the roots of what happened in Nazi Germany. And they are there in *every* human being.
>
> As I recognized – more clearly than ever before – that I myself stood in desperate need of forgiveness, I was able to forgive, and finally I felt completely free.

Josef Ben-Eliezer, another friend, had a similar journey. Born in Frankfurt, Germany, in 1929, he is the son of Polish Jews who fled their homeland to escape persecution and poverty, but found little respite from either:

My first memory of anti-Semitism is from when I was three years old. I was standing at the window of our house on the Ostendstrasse when a formation of Hitler Youth marched past, singing *Wenn Judenblut vom Messer spritzt* ("When Jewish blood runs from our knives"). I still remember the horror on my parents' faces.

Our family soon decided to leave the country, and by the end of 1933 we had moved back to Rozwadow, Poland. Most of its inhabitants were Jews: artisans, tailors, carpenters, and merchants. There was a great deal of poverty, but under the circumstances we were considered middle-class. We lived in Rozwadow for the next six years.

In 1939 the war started, and within weeks the Germans entered our town. My father and older brother hid in the attic, and whenever someone knocked at our door and asked for them, we said they were not at home.

Then came the dreaded public announcement: all Jews had to gather in the town square. We were given only a few hours. We took whatever we could carry in bundles on our backs. From the square, the SS forced us to march toward a river several miles from the village. Uniformed men rode alongside us on motorcycles. One of them stopped and shouted at us to hurry up, then came up to my father and struck him.

At the riverbank other uniformed men were waiting for us. They searched us for money, jewelry, and watches – they did not find the sum of money my parents had hidden in my little sister's clothing – and then ordered us to cross the river, into a no-man's-land. They did not instruct us what to do after that, so we found lodging in a nearby village.

A few days later we suddenly heard that the far side of the river was also going to be occupied by the Germans. We panicked, and with the money we had hidden, my parents – together with two or three other families – bought a horse and wagon to carry the younger children and what little we had managed to bring along on our backs.

We traveled east toward Russia, hoping to reach the border before dark, but found ourselves in a large forest when night fell. During the night we were attacked by armed thugs who demanded we hand over everything we had. It was a frightening moment, but luckily the men in our caravan had the courage to resist them, and in the end our attackers left, taking only a bicycle and a few other small items.

Josef spent the next years in Siberia, from where he escaped to Palestine in 1943. After the war he met Jews who had survived the concentration camps:

When the first children freed from Bergen-Belsen and Buchenwald began to arrive in Palestine in 1945, I was horrified to hear what they had gone through. They were young boys – twelve, thirteen, and fourteen years old – but they looked like old men. I was devastated, and filled with hatred for the Nazis...

Then the British began to restrict the immigration of Holocaust survivors to Palestine, and I was filled with hatred for them too. Like other Jews, I promised myself that I would never again go like a sheep to slaughter, at least not without putting up a good fight. We felt we were living in a world of wild beasts, and we couldn't see how we would survive unless we became like them.

When the British mandate in Palestine came to an end, we no longer had them to fight, but we did have the Arabs, who wanted "our" land. That was when I joined the army. I could no longer allow myself to be trampled on…

During one campaign, my unit forced a group of Palestinians to leave their village within hours. We didn't allow them to leave in peace, but turned on them out of sheer hatred. While interrogating them, we beat them brutally and even murdered some of them. We had not been ordered to do this but acted on our own initiative. Our lowest instincts had been released.

Suddenly, my childhood in wartime Poland flashed before my eyes. In my mind I relived my own experience as a ten-year-old, driven from my home. Here, too, were people – men, women, and children – fleeing with whatever they could carry. And there was fear in their eyes, a fear that I myself knew all too well. I was terribly distressed, but I was under orders, and I continued to search them for valuables…

Josef was no longer a victim, but his new position on the side of power brought him no peace. In fact, it did the opposite. Again and again, the memory of his own suffering ate at him and brought new waves of guilt.

Josef left the army, but he still wasn't happy. He abandoned Judaism, and then religion as a whole. He tried to make sense of the world by rationalizing its evils. But even that didn't seem to work. It was only through his discovery of the "real" Jesus, he says – "someone who has very little to do with all the violence that is carried out in his name" – that he realized the freedom of a life lived without hatred.

> In my heart I heard Jesus' words, "How often did I want to gather you, and you would not." I felt the power of these words and knew that it could unite people across every barrier – people of all nations, races, and religions. It was an overwhelming experience. It turned my life upside down, because I realized that it meant the healing of hatred, and the forgiveness of sins.
>
> In my new faith, I have experienced the reality of forgiveness. And I ask myself, "How, then, can you not forgive others?"

Jared, Hela, and Josef had more than enough reason to withhold forgiveness. The burdens they carried were, at least initially, the result of other people's prejudices and hatreds, not their own. In a sense, they had every right to feel the way they did. Yet as soon as they were able to see themselves as fallible human beings, they were able to lay aside their self-justification. And in making the conscious decision to break the cycle of hatred, they discovered their ability to forgive.

4

Bless Your Persecutors

At some thoughts one stands perplexed — especially at the
sight of men's sin — and wonders whether one should use
force or humble love. Always decide to use humble love. If
you resolve to do that, once and for all, you can subdue the
whole world. Loving humility is marvelously strong, the
strongest of all things, and there is nothing else like it.

FYODOR DOSTOEVSKY

In the well-known passage of the Gospels called the Sermon on the Mount, Jesus teaches us to love our enemies –
in fact, to "bless" those who persecute us. But it wasn't just
a sermon. As his unmistakably compassionate plea from
the cross shows – "Father, forgive them, for they know not
what they do" – he practiced what he preached. So did
Stephen, the first Christian martyr, who prayed much the
same thing as he was being stoned to death: "Father, do
not hold this against them."

Many people dismiss such an attitude as self-destructive foolishness. How and why should we embrace someone intent on harming or killing us? Why not fight back in self-defense? When I showed an early manuscript of this book to Mumia Abu-Jamal, an African-American writer and friend, he reacted in just this way:

> I cannot imagine myself ever asking the oppressed – whether Jews, Native Americans, or any other persecuted peoples throughout history – to forgive their oppressors. Who can dare?
>
> I hear you answer: "Jesus!" But when I look at the Jews, I see that it was precisely the followers of Jesus – so-called "Christians" – who became their deadliest enemies, who herded them into the ghettoes of Europe, and when the ghettoes filled, into the ovens of Auschwitz, while millions of Christians stood by in silence. As for the Native Americans, this nation pushed them to the edge of extinction, herded them into reservations, onto the worst lands.
>
> It's easy for folks who live in a virtual paradise, who have enough to eat, farms, land, nice homes, businesses, etc., to preach about forgiveness. But is it really fair to say that to people who live in hellholes – jobless, threatened by imminent death by starvation – people who are, as Frantz Fanon put it, "the wretched of the earth?" Are they to forgive the fat, well-fed millions who voted for their starvation? Who voted for war? Who voted for prisons? Who voted for their perpetual repression? Who wish,

in their heart-of-hearts, that they were never born? Should they forgive them for the repression to come? For the genocide that is to come?

"Lord, forgive them for what they do, even though they and their ancestors have been doing it for five hundred years..." Can your heart embrace such a prayer?

It is for this reason that my heart has been called to political action: to change hellish realities, and to try to transform this world from the hell it is for billions of her inhabitants. Change those conditions, and then perhaps forgiveness can be born.

Mumia's words may seem overly harsh to some, but they are significant because they come from a perspective unlike that of anyone else in this book. For the last eighteen years he has sat on Pennsylvania's death row serving time for a murder that I (and thousands of others both here in the United States and abroad) believe he did not commit.

Like Mumia, Raja Shehadeh, a Palestinian human rights lawyer, is no stranger to repression, but he takes a very different view of the matter:

For me, the act of forgiveness carries a lot of power. It is an assertion of one's dignity to have the means and ability to forgive...It may be difficult to understand, because it turns conventional logic on its head, but idealistically speaking, I think that if there is to be peace, there has to be forgiveness...

Though misunderstood and ridiculed, Raja's understanding of forgiveness is not entirely unusual – it has been embraced by hundreds of persecuted minorities throughout history, from the earliest Christian believers, to the Anabaptists of the radical Reformation, to our century's followers of Tolstoy, Gandhi, and Martin Luther King.

It is probably best explained in this passage from King's book *Strength to Love:*

> Probably no admonition of Jesus has been more difficult to follow than the command to love our enemies. Some people have sincerely felt that its actual practice is not possible. It is easy, they say, to love those who love you, but how can one love those who openly and insidiously seek to defeat you…?
>
> Far from being the pious injunction of a Utopian dreamer, the command to love one's enemy is an absolute necessity for our survival. Love even for our enemies is the key to the solution of the problems of our world. Jesus is not an impractical idealist; he is the practical realist…
>
> Returning hate for hate multiplies hate, adding deeper darkness to a night already devoid of stars. Darkness cannot drive out darkness; only light can do that. Hate cannot drive out hate; only love can do that. Hate multiplies hate, violence multiplies violence, and toughness multiplies toughness in a descending spiral of destruction…
>
> Love is the only force capable of transforming an enemy into a friend. We never get rid of an enemy by meet-

ing hate with hate; we get rid of an enemy by getting rid of enmity. By its very nature, hate destroys and tears down; by its very nature, love creates and builds up. Love transforms with redemptive power.

King's commitment to love as a political weapon grew out of his faith, but there was a good streak of pragmatism in his thinking as well. He knew that he and other African-Americans involved in the civil rights movement would have to live for decades to come with the same people they were now confronting. If they let their treatment embitter them, it would soon lead to violence, which would only lead to new cycles of repression and embitterment. Rather than breaking down the walls of racial hatred, it would build them higher. Only by forgiving their oppressors, King said, could African-Americans end the "descending spiral of destruction." Only forgiveness could bring about lasting change:

> We must develop and maintain the capacity to forgive. Whoever is devoid of the power to forgive is devoid of the power to love. It is impossible even to begin the act of loving one's enemies without the prior acceptance of the necessity, over and over again, of forgiving those who inflict evil and injury upon us.
>
> It is also necessary to realize that the forgiving act must always be initiated by the person who has been wronged, the victim of some great hurt, the recipient of some tortuous injustice, the absorber of some terrible act of op-

pression. The wrongdoer may request forgiveness. They may come to themselves, and like the prodigal son, move up some dusty road, their heart palpitating with the desire for forgiveness. But only the injured neighbor, the loving father back home, can really pour out the warm waters of forgiveness.

Forgiveness does not mean ignoring what has been done or putting a false label on an evil act. It means, rather, that the evil act no longer remains as a barrier to the relationship. Forgiveness is a catalyst creating the atmosphere necessary for a fresh start and a new beginning...

To our most bitter opponents we say: We shall match your capacity to inflict suffering by our capacity to endure suffering. We shall meet your physical force with soul force. Do to us what you will, and we shall continue to love you.

We cannot in all good conscience obey your unjust laws, because noncooperation with evil is as much a moral obligation as is cooperation with good. Throw us in jail, and we shall still love you. Send your hooded perpetrators of violence into our community at the midnight hour and beat us and leave us half dead, and we shall still love you. But be ye assured that we will wear you down by our capacity to suffer.

One day we shall win our freedom, but not only for ourselves. We shall so appeal to your heart and conscience that we shall win you in the process, and our victory will be a double victory.

In the spring of 1965 I marched with King in Marion, Alabama, and experienced firsthand his deep love and humility in the face of injustice. I was visiting the Tuskegee Institute with colleagues from New York when we heard about the death of Jimmie Lee Jackson, a young man who had been shot eight days earlier when a rally at a church in Marion was broken up by police. State troopers from all over central Alabama had converged on the town and beaten the protesters with clubs as they poured out onto the streets.

Bystanders later described a scene of utter chaos: white onlookers smashed cameras and shot out street lights, while police officers brutally attacked black men and women, some of whom were kneeling and praying on the steps of their church.

Jimmie's crime was to tackle a state trooper who was mercilessly beating his mother. His punishment: to be shot in the stomach and clubbed over the head until almost dead. Denied admission at the local hospital, he was taken to Selma, where he was able to tell his story to reporters. He died several days later.

At the news of Jimmie's death, we drove to Selma immediately. The viewing, at Brown Chapel, was open-casket, and although the mortician had done his best to cover his injuries, the wounds on Jimmie's head could not be hidden: three murderous blows, each an inch wide and three inches long, ran above his ear, at the base of his skull, and on the top of his head.

Deeply shaken, we attended a memorial service there. The room was packed with about three thousand people (many more stood outside), and we sat on a window sill at the back. We never heard one note of anger or revenge in the service. Instead, a spirit of courage emanated from the men and women of the congregation, especially as they rose to sing the old slave song, "Ain't gonna let nobody turn me 'round."

Later, at a second service in Marion, the atmosphere was decidedly more subdued. Lining the veranda of the county court house across the street stood a long row of state troopers, hands on their night sticks, looking straight at us. These were the same men who had attacked Marion's blacks only days before. The crowd of whites gathered at nearby City Hall was no less intimidating. Armed with binoculars and cameras, they scanned and photographed us so thoroughly that we felt every one of us had been marked.

Afterwards, at the cemetery, King spoke about forgiveness and love. He pleaded with his people to pray for the police, to forgive the murderer, and to forgive those who were persecuting them. Then we held hands and sang, "We shall overcome." It was an unforgettable moment. If there was ever cause for hatred or vengeance, it was here. But none was to be felt, not even from Jimmie's parents.

Not long ago I read about a remarkable act of forgiveness by the children of Selma in those same days of early 1965. Local students had organized a peaceful after-school march when the town's notorious Sheriff Clark arrived. Clark's deputies began to push and prod the children, and soon they were running. Initially the boys and girls thought the sheriff was marching them toward the county jail, but it soon became clear that they were headed for a prison camp almost five miles out of town. The men did not relent until the children were retching and vomiting. Later they claimed they wanted to wear out Selma's "marching fever" for good.

A few days after this incident, Sheriff Clark was hospitalized with chest pains. Unbelievably, Selma's school children organized a second march outside the court house, chanting prayers for his recovery and carrying get-well signs.

Eminent child psychiatrist Robert Coles observed the same remarkable attitude of forgiveness among children when he was working in a New Orleans hospital in 1960. White parents, openly opposed to a federal court decision that ended segregation in the city's schools, not only withdrew their children from any school that admitted blacks, but picketed these schools as well.

One child, six-year-old Ruby Bridges, was the sole African American student at her school, which meant that for a while she was also the only student there. For weeks she had to be escorted to school by federal marshals. One day, her teacher saw her mouthing words as she passed the lines of angry white parents hurling abuse. When the teacher reported this to Coles, he was curious: What had she said?

When asked, Ruby said that she had been praying for the parents of her white classmates. Coles was perplexed. "But why?" "Because they need praying for," she answered. She had heard in church about Jesus' dying words, "Father, forgive them, for they know not what they do," and had taken them to heart.

Through James Christensen, the prior of a Trappist monastery in Rome, I recently learned of a remarkable story of someone who not only forgave his persecutors, but did so before the fact. In May 1996, the GIA, a radical Islamic group in Algeria, kidnapped seven of James's fellow Trappists in the Atlas Mountains and threatened to hold them hostage until France released several of their own imprisoned compatriots. When the French government refused, the GIA slit the monks' throats.

All France was horrified, and every Catholic church in France tolled its bells at the same time in the monks' memory. What struck me most about the tragedy, however, was something that had quietly foreshadowed it two years before. The prior of the Algerian monastery, Christian de Chergé, had had a strange premonition that he would soon die a violent death, and wrote a letter forgiving his future assassins. He sealed the letter and left it with his mother in France. Opened only after his murder, it read in part:

> If it should happen one day – and it could be today – that I become a victim of the terrorism that now seems to encompass all the foreigners living in Algeria, I would like my community, my church, my family, to remember that my life was given to God and to Algeria; and that they accept that the sole Master of all life was not a stranger to this brutal departure.
>
> I would like, when the time comes, to have a space of clearness that would allow me to beg forgiveness of God and of my fellow human beings, and at the same time to forgive with all my heart the one who will strike me down.
>
> I could not desire such a death; it seems to me important to state this: How could I rejoice if the Algerian people I love were indiscriminately accused of my murder?

My death, obviously, will appear to confirm those who hastily judged me naïve or idealistic: "Let him tell us now what he thinks of it!" But they should know that…for this life lost, I give thanks to God. In this "thank you," which is said for everything in my life from now on, I certainly include you, my last-minute friend who will not have known what you are doing…I commend you to the God in whose face I see yours. And may we find each other, happy "good thieves" in Paradise, if it please God, the Father of us both.

Like so many others on both sides of the Arab-Israeli conflict, Bishara Awad, a Palestinian acquaintance of mine, has been wounded by his share of injustices. Speaking recently about his life-long struggle to forgive, he told me:

> In 1948, during the terrible war between the Arabs and the Jewish settlers, thousands of Palestinians died and many more became homeless. Our own family was not spared. My father was shot dead by a stray bullet, and there was no decent burial place. No one could leave the area for fear of getting shot at by either side; there was not a priest nor a minister to say a prayer. So Mother read to us from the Bible, and the men who were present buried my father in the courtyard. There was no way they could have taken him to the regular cemetery in the city.
>
> Mother thus became a widow at the age of twenty-nine, and she was left with seven children. I was only nine

years old. For weeks we were caught up in the crossfire and were unable to leave our basement room. Then one night, the Jordanian army forced us to run to the Old City. That was the last time we ever saw our home and our furniture. We ran away with nothing but the clothes on our backs, some of us only in pajamas…

In the Old City we were refugees. We were put in a kerosene storage room that had no furniture. A Muslim family gave us some blankets and some food. Life was very hard; I still remember nights when we went to sleep without any food.

Mother had been trained as a nurse, and she got a job at a hospital for $25 a month. She worked at night and continued her studies during the day, and we children were put in orphanages.

My sisters were accepted in a Muslim school, and we boys were placed in a home run by a British woman. To me, this was a real blow. First I had lost my father, and now I was away from my mother and my family. We were allowed to visit home once a month, but otherwise we stayed at the boys' home for the next twelve years. Here, with my two brothers and eighty other boys, my suffering continued. We never had enough to eat. The food was terrible and the treatment harsh.

As an adult, Bishara went to school in the United States and became an American citizen. Later he returned to Israel and took a job teaching in a Christian school. Looking back, he says:

That first year I was very frustrated. I did not accomplish much and I felt defeated...There was mounting hatred against the Jewish oppressors: all of my students were Palestinians, and all had suffered in the same way I had...I wasn't able to help my students, because of the overriding hatred in me. I had harbored it since childhood without even realizing it.

One night I prayed to God in tears. I asked forgiveness for hating the Jews and for allowing hatred to control my life...Instantly he took away my frustration, hopelessness, and hatred and replaced it with love.

In a culture that emphasizes self-preservation and individualism, forgiveness is scoffed at so routinely that most people never stop to consider its potential to heal wounds such as the ones Bishara described. But neither do they consider the fruits of its alternative, which is bitterness.

Naim Ateek, a well-known Palestinian priest in Jerusalem whose father lost everything he had to the Israeli Army in 1948, says:

When people hate, its power engulfs them and they are totally consumed by it...Keep struggling against hatred and resentment. At times you will have the upper hand, at times you will feel beaten down. Although it is extremely difficult, never let hatred completely overtake you...

Never stop trying to live the commandment of love and forgiveness. Do not dilute the strength of Jesus's message; do not shun it; do not dismiss it as unreal and impractical. Do not cut it to your size, trying to make it more applicable to real life in the world. Do not change it so that it will suit you. Keep it as it is, aspire to it, desire it, and work for its achievement.

Far from leaving us weak and vulnerable, forgiveness is empowering, both to the person who grants it and the one who receives it. In bringing true closure to the most difficult situations, it allows us to lay aside the riddles of retribution and human fairness, and to experience true peace of heart. Finally, it sets into motion a positive chain reaction that passes on the fruits of our forgiveness to others.

5

Forgiveness and Justice

Truth without love kills, but love without truth lies.

EBERHARD ARNOLD

David, an Israeli acquaintance, experienced hardships similar to those of Hela and Josef, in Chapter 3, but offers a somewhat different viewpoint. David's story raises an age-old question posed by generations of suffering men and women over the course of human history: Are there no limits to forgiveness?

I was born in Kassel, Germany, in 1929, the fateful year of the financial and economic crash that had such a decisive impact on world affairs and was instrumental in bringing the Nazis to power in Germany...My father was a journalist; mother an educator. Our family was well off, and life was happy until the clouds of fascism began to accumulate.

Like many Jews throughout the country, father did not take the Nazis too seriously at first. How could the solid, cultured Germans fall for that nonsense? But when Hitler became chancellor, well-wishing friends advised my parents to leave Germany.

So my father took leave of his beloved homeland, where he was born and raised, and for which he had fought in the First World War. Mother and I followed shortly, and we were reunited in Strasbourg, just over the French border. We took with us only a few of our possessions. It was the end of our normal, accustomed way of life; we had become homeless, wandering Jews, without a nationality and without rights.

For me, a curious three-year-old, it was an exciting time. I quickly learned new customs, a new language, and I made new friends. But a year later we had to move again; as German refugees, we were considered a security risk in border areas. We went to a village in the Vosges – another change. My parents had to learn new trades and a new language, to adapt to a very different culture, to do without most of the comforts of their previous lifestyle – and before that, to make a living under difficult circumstances...

A year later, the factory that employed my mother burned down, which necessitated another move, this time to Marseille. Again my parents tried to eke out a living, and they built up a rather precarious existence. We frequently changed apartments, which meant I frequently had to change schools and friends. I never had the chance to form lasting relationships...

Then the Second World War broke out, and everything went to pieces. I was a stranger again, and an alien one on top of that…France was invaded and then occupied by the German army, and soon the Gestapo were making arrests…Our apartment and my parents' business were confiscated but, with the help of French friends, we went into hiding.

Finally my parents decided that our only hope of survival lay in escaping over the Pyrenees to Spain. After walking for three days through snow-covered mountains, the Spanish *Guardia Civil* (border police) caught up with us. Luckily they let us through – as they did most of the nearly 10,000 Jews who illegally crossed into Spain. Had we been shipped back to France, it would have meant sure death…

As it was, we were torn apart at the Gerona police station. Father was sent to a camp in Miranda-del-Ebro, and mother to the local prison. I was left behind on my own. I spent the most miserable night of my life alone in a freezing cell, thinking I had lost my parents forever. The next day I landed in Gerona's orphanage, which did little to improve my spirits. There I turned thirteen (the age Jewish boys are received into the congregation of the faithful) – and missed my *bar-mitzvah*…

After a few months I was sent to join my mother, and together we were transferred to a prison in Madrid. Later the whole family was reunited, and in 1944, with the assistance of the Jewish Joint Welfare Committee, we were able to move to Palestine.

In spite of all the suffering the Germans caused my family and my people, I still feel attached to their history and culture, which I absorbed through my parents. I have done my best to recreate links with decent Germans. Still, I can never forget the six million Jews – including 1.5 million innocent children – who were tortured and exterminated by the Nazis and their helpers.

If forgiving means renouncing blind hatred and feelings of revenge – yes, then it is possible. I forgive those who stood by helplessly, and those who did not dare to speak up. I know how much courage it takes to stand up to authority and to oppose the kind of terror the Nazis imposed. But what about the monsters who committed the worst atrocities in human memory?

Is it possible to forgive Hitler and his henchmen, his SS commanders and soldiers, his death-camp guards, his Gestapo officials? Is it possible to forgive torturers and murderers who starved, machine-gunned, and gassed hundreds of thousands of helpless men, women, and children? Are there no limits to forgiveness?

David's question is, I think, not motivated by resentment toward the exterminators of his people, but by a fear that forgiving them would somehow spell exoneration. As someone committed to doing what he can to ensure that similar atrocities never happen again, he cannot bring himself to release them of their responsibility and guilt.

And he shouldn't. Who could ever take it upon himself to excuse a man like Hitler? But forgiveness is not about excusing or exonerating people, nor is it about weighing the morality – or immorality – of their actions.

Writing in 1947, when the full horrors of the Holocaust had only just come to light, C. S. Lewis wrote, "There is all the difference in the world between forgiving and excusing." Most people, he suggested, don't like to admit when they've done something wrong, so they make excuses for their actions. (In the case of the Nazis, thousands of Germans said after the fall of the Third Reich that they were "only following orders.") Instead of asking for forgiveness, they try to get others to accept their excuses and "extenuating circumstances," and to see that they aren't really to blame. But, Lewis continued, "if one is not really to blame, then there is nothing to forgive. In that sense forgiveness and excusing are almost opposites."

> Real forgiveness means looking steadily at the sin, the sin that is left over without any excuse, after all allowances have been made, and seeing it in all its horror, dirt, meanness and malice, and nevertheless being wholly reconciled to the person who has done it. That, and only that, is forgiveness.

While witnessing the beating of a young man by sheriff's deputies from the Los Angeles Police Department, Roberto Rodriguez decided to photograph them. Before he knew it, he was attacked by the same club-wielding officers. Hospitalized with a cracked skull, he was then jailed and charged with attempting to kill the officers who almost took his life.

Roberto, now a nationally syndicated columnist, fought back, and after seven long years, he won both an acquittal and a federal civil rights lawsuit. In the meantime, however, his attempts to challenge the system made him a marked man:

> Once during this time I was handcuffed to a bench in a police station, with my picture posted over me, and an article detailing my legal battle with the police department. Each officer who passed by was told not to forget who I was. Apparently they didn't, because during the next few years I was continually harassed – and arrested about sixty times.

Ask Roberto what he thinks about forgiving, and he has answers. But he has plenty of questions, too.

> You ask me about forgiveness? Do I need to forgive the deputies who beat me, who made me believe – in the middle of the night – that they were driving me to my final destination? Do I need to forgive the officers who falsely arrested me and relentlessly pursued me, the district attorney who filed charges against me, the prosecutors who tried to put me away? Do I need to forgive the politicians who wouldn't touch me with a ten-foot pole

when I pleaded with them for help, or the reporters who painted me as a criminal? And what about my own lawyer, who abandoned my case two days before trial?

I realize that we cannot be fully human if we have hatred within us – if we are consumed by anger or harbor resentment. These emotions define our lives. Especially for someone who has been brutalized and dehumanized, getting rid of these debilitating emotions is fundamental to healing. But doing that also means searching for something else to fill the void: searching for what it actually means to be human.

I began that search in 1998, on my birthday, when I sang for the first time in almost thirty years. A few months later, I started to paint, and then to write fiction. I had finally begun to regain my humanity.

I still haven't completely recovered from my trauma, but at least I can smile, laugh, and love life once again, and I can make others laugh and smile. I sing at rest homes and senior centers. I arrived at this through my pursuit of justice, though also through prayer and meditation.

Though thousands of minorities suffer similar mistreatment, most are not so fortunate as Roberto. Most never see justice served. Should they too be expected to forgive their oppressors? Roberto thinks they must, and not only for their own sake:

Because these abuses continue year after year, there is a lot of bitterness on America's streets, especially among those who have been brutalized and falsely imprisoned. Some are zombies. Others are walking time-bombs, filled with hate and ready to explode. And they do explode. Look what happened in Los Angeles in 1992, after the Rodney King verdict. Tragically, such outrage usually hurts the very people it is supposed to avenge: family, friends and neighbors.

All this is not a personal tragedy, but a societal one. It is like an out-of-control disease. Far from being a cure, forgiveness is in this realm a luxury at best. Yet precisely because there continue to be such gross injustices, those who have been dehumanized need to forgive – to heal on their own, without waiting for apologies. Forgiveness does not require apologies.

Of course this does not mean simply folding one's arms and going merrily home, oblivious of ongoing injustices. It simply means that as one struggles to regain one's humanity and fights for one's rights, one can do so without anger, hatred, and bitterness.

To be more specific: forgiving one's brutalizers may help them toward becoming more human. But it is only part of the solution. As a society, we have learned that people who commit acts of violence such as torturing or killing others need more than forgiveness if they are to be prevented from committing similar crimes again. They need to be treated. A brutalizer will never find true peace until he exorcises his own demons.

After Louisiana businessman Bill Chadwick lost his son, Michael, to a drunk driver, he "wanted to see justice done." Like Roberto, however, he discovered that justice alone couldn't bring him the closure he was looking for.

My twenty-one-year-old son Michael was killed instantly on October 23, 1993, in a car crash. His best friend, who was in the back seat, was also killed. The driver, who had been drinking heavily and was speeding recklessly, received minor injuries; he was subsequently charged with two counts of vehicular homicide. Michael had only a trace of alcohol in his system, and his best friend had none.

The wheels of justice grind very slowly. The courts took more than a year to find the case against the driver. We attended hearing after hearing, and each time the case was delayed. There was even an attempt by the defense attorney to discredit the findings of the blood-alcohol tests, although this was unsuccessful. Finally, the defendant pleaded guilty and was sentenced to six years per count, to be served concurrently.

We suggested to the probation office that a boot camp-style program might be of benefit to him – we really weren't out to hurt him, but we believed he needed to pay for what he had done. All the same, we received a pretty ugly letter from his mother suggesting that we had somehow pushed for the maximum sentence. She said that if it had been her son who died, with Michael driving, she would not have held a grudge. I suggested that until her son were actually dead, she should not talk about what she would or wouldn't do.

Her son was finally sentenced to six months in boot camp, with the rest of his six-year sentence to be served on intensive parole. In six months, her son was coming home. Ours was not.

I guess I had bought into the belief that, somehow, things would be different after the driver had been brought to justice. I think that is what people mean when they talk about "closure." We think that if there is someone to blame, then we can put the matter to rest; because then the victim will get some sort of justice, and the pain will finally go away. In the years since Michael's death, I have read countless accounts of bereaved people who are looking for closure of this sort. I have also seen them on Oprah, shouting for the death penalty, as if having the perpetrator dead would somehow help.

I was angry at the driver, of course. But I was angry at Michael, too. After all, he had made some really bad decisions that night; he had put his life in jeopardy. I had to go through this anger in order to come to grips with my feelings. However, even after the sentencing, I did not find closure. What I did find was a big hole in my soul – and nothing to fill it with.

It was some months later that it hit me: until I could forgive the driver, I would never find the closure I was looking for. Forgiving was different from removing responsibility. The driver was still responsible for Michael's death, but I had to forgive him before I could let the incident go. No amount of punishment could ever even the score. I had to be willing to forgive without the score being even. And this process of forgiveness did not really involve the driver – it involved me. It was a process that I had to go through; I had to change, no matter what he did.

The road to forgiveness was long and painful. I had to forgive more than just the driver. I had to forgive Michael, and God (for allowing it to happen), and myself. Ultimately, it was forgiving myself that was the most difficult. There were many times in my own life I had driven Michael places when I myself was under the influence of alcohol. That was a hard recognition – my need to forgive myself. My anger at other people was just my own fear turned outward. I had projected my own guilt onto others – the driver, the courts, God, Michael – so that I would not have to look at myself. And it wasn't until I could see my part in this that my outlook could change.

This is what I learned: that the closure we seek comes in forgiving. And this closure is really up to us, because the power to forgive does not lie outside us, but within.

In a society like ours, where victim's rights are increasingly seen as unassailable, Bill's insights are not popular ones. For many people, even vindication by a court is no longer enough. They want a personal role in the act of retribution. In several states, murder victims' families are offered spots in the witness rooms of execution chambers, or the opportunity to make statements at sentencing.

Not long ago I read that at the sentencing of Kip Kinkel, a fifteen-year-old who went on a shooting spree in Springfield, Oregon, in 1998, family members of his victims grew so angry that the judge had to cut them off and call the court to order. At one especially chilling moment, the mother of one victim spoke of her agony, and said with unabashed relish that she hoped Kip would be tortured by it in the same way she was – for the rest of his life. "That, for me, is the ultimate justice."

However justified this woman's quest might seem, it is a fruitless one. Blinded by her grief – and determined to make the person responsible for it share it with her – she is seeking solace in a place she will never find it: revenge. Though my heart goes out to her, it is clear to me that she will never find healing, but only further heartache and deep disillusionment.

Even when the path to forgiveness is daunting or steep, that does not mean it is impossible. In spring 1998, Carroll and Doris King – friends of mine from Pennsylvania – traveled to Iraq with a human rights delegation to examine the effects of the UN sanctions there. While in Baghdad they met Ghaidaa, a woman who had suffered more than any mother I had ever heard of, but was still ready to forgive those who had hurt her.

Ghaidaa lost nine children in the destruction of Al Amariyah, a massive, reinforced concrete shelter in Baghdad that was penetrated by American "smart bombs" during the Gulf War. More than one thousand Iraqi civilians were incinerated in the bombing, most of them women and children.

Today, Ghaidaa leads tourists among the shelter ruins, hoping that those who see its horrors – among other things, ghostly silhouettes were left wherever human bodies shielded the walls from the extreme heat – will speak out against future bombings. After taking one of Ghaidaa's tours, Carroll and Doris, stunned, asked her to forgive them for what America had done to her family and people. A former Air Force officer who had flown bombing sorties over Europe in World War II, Carroll especially felt he bore a share of the guilt. Shaking his hand, then hugging Doris and bursting into tears, Ghaidaa cried, "I forgive you."

Ghaidaa will never find "justice" on human terms. How can one ever replace nine dead children? She will certainly never be able to forget them. But in finding the hearts of two people who asked her to forgive them, she has found something much greater.

6

The Deeds of Mercy

Though justice be thy plea, consider this:
That in the course of justice none of us
Should see salvation. We do pray for mercy,
And that same prayer doth teach us all to render
The deeds of mercy.

WILLIAM SHAKESPEARE

In his novel *Too Late the Phalarope,* Alan Paton writes of a respected man who commits what his society sees as an unpardonable sin: adultery. When the affair is brought to light, the man's family is devastated. His friends leave him, his relatives spurn him, and his father dies in shame. Yet a neighbor agonizes over the incident: "An offender can be punished," he says. "But to punish and not to restore, that is the greatest of all offenses…If a man takes unto himself God's right to punish, then he must also take upon himself God's promise to restore."

If there is anything that reveals the apparent contradictions of the mystery we call forgiveness, it is this thorny "offense." Most of us find it difficult to let go even of relatively small grudges, yet restoration or reconciliation – call it what you will – demands not only that, but the active attempt to embrace a person whom it would be far easier to avoid.

When Miami native Chris Carrier was ten, a former family employee abducted him, assaulted him, shot him in the head, and left him to die in the Florida Everglades. But that isn't the end of the story:

> Friday, December 20, 1974, was no ordinary day. It was the last day of school before the Christmas holidays, and we got out early.
>
> I stepped off the bus at 1:15 P.M. and began to walk home. An older-looking man who happened to be walking towards me on the sidewalk appeared to recognize me. Just two houses away from home, he introduced himself as a friend of my father. He told me he was hosting a party for my father and asked if I would help him with some decorations.
>
> I agreed and walked back up the street with him to the local youth center where he had parked his motor home. Once inside the vehicle, I put down my things and made myself comfortable.

The Miami I knew quickly disappeared as he drove north. In an area removed from suburban traffic, he stopped on the side of the road. He claimed that he had missed a turn. He handed me a map, instructing me to look for a certain number, and went into the back of the motor home "to get something."

As I studied the map and waited, I felt a quick sting in the shoulder, and then another. I turned around to see him standing behind me with an ice pick in his hand. Then he pulled me out of my seat and onto the floor. Kneeling over me, he stabbed me in the chest several times. I pleaded with him to stop and promised him that if he would let me go, I wouldn't say anything.

I was immeasurably relieved when he stood up. He told me that he was going to drop me off somewhere, after which he would call my father and let him know where I was. He allowed me to sit in the back of the motor home as he drove. Yet I was painfully aware that this situation was beyond my control. When I asked him why he was doing this to me, he said that my father had "cost him a great deal of money."

After driving for another hour or so, he turned onto a dusty side road. He told me this was where my father would pick me up. We walked out together into the bushes and I sat down where he told me I should sit. The last thing I remembered was him walking away.

Six days later, the evening of December 26, Chris was found by a local deer hunter. His head was bloody and his eyes were black. He had been shot through the head.

Miraculously, there was no brain damage, but he didn't remember being shot.

In the years that followed, Chris struggled daily with the insecurity of knowing that his abductor was still at large.

> Everywhere I went, the fear of what was around the corner, what was lurking in the shadows, haunted me. I was alarmed by every noise and motion. Was that a dog? What was that – is it really just the wind? What was that creak in the next room? Was someone coming in our back door? For three years I spent every night without fail in a sleeping bag at the foot of my parents' bed.

Chris also had to come to terms with the physical limitations caused by his injuries: he was now blind in one eye and could no longer take part in contact sports. And as any teenager would, he worried about his appearance.

Chris resented public mention of his survival, and remembers wondering how this "miracle" could have left him so miserable. Then, at the age of thirteen, he underwent a change, and began to see his nightmare differently. He realized his injuries could have been much worse – in fact, he could have died. He also recognized that staying angry would never change anything. He decided to stop feeling sorry for himself, and to get on with his life instead.

Then, on September 3, 1996, Chris received a telephone call that changed his life once again. It was a detective from the Coral Gables police department, and he was calling to notify him that an elderly man at a local nursing home, David McAllister, had confessed to being his abductor. (He was, though in the eyes of the law there was never enough evidence to bring him to trial.) David had worked as an aide for an elderly uncle in the Carrier family, but had been fired on account of his drinking problems. Chris visited David the following day.

It was an awkward moment, walking into his room, but as soon as I saw him I was overwhelmed with compassion. The man I found was not an intimidating kidnapper, but a frail seventy-seven-year-old who had been blind for the last half-dozen years.

David's body was ruined by alcoholism and smoking – he weighed little more than sixty pounds. He had no family, or if he did, they wanted nothing to do with him, and no friends. The only material possessions he had were some pictures that kids in a nearby elementary school had drawn for him. David had a roommate, but they didn't even know each other or communicate. Here was a man who faced death with only his regrets to keep him company.

When I first spoke to David, he was rather callous. I suppose he thought I was a police officer. A friend who had accompanied me wisely asked him a few simple questions that led to him admitting that he had abducted me. He then asked, "Did you ever wish you could tell that young boy that you were sorry for what you did?"

David answered emphatically, "I wish I could." That was when I introduced myself to him.

Unable to see, David clasped my hand and told me he was sorry for what he had done to me. As he did, I looked down at him, and it came over me like a wave: Why should anyone have to face death without family, friends, the joy of life – without hope? I couldn't do anything but offer him my forgiveness and friendship.

In the days that followed this dramatic meeting, Chris began to visit David as often as he could, usually bringing along his wife, Leslie, and their two daughters. The two men spent hours talking, reading, and even praying together, and as they did, the old man's hardness gradually melted away.

Throughout that week I shared with him about the victories of my recovery, and about my life since the horrifying day he had tried to kill me. I'd graduated from high school, from college, and then from grad school. I had married; I had a beautiful wife and family. I shared these things with him so that he could understand, in the way the ancient Israelite Joseph tried to get his brothers to understand, after they had abandoned him, "That which you intended for evil, God has used for good." I let him know that he had not ruined my life, in the end, and that there was nothing between us now.

Three weeks later, just hours after Chris had tucked his ailing friend into bed for the night, David died.

Chris says it wasn't hard for him to forgive, though the reporters who later took interest in his story still don't understand how or why he did it. They admire his ability to forgive, but cannot understand what compelled him. They always go blank when the subject of forgiveness comes up, he says, and seem more comfortable focusing on the drama of his abduction and the details of his torture. But Chris knows why he forgave David:

> There is a very pragmatic reason for forgiving. When we are wronged, we can either respond by seeking revenge, or we can forgive. If we choose revenge, our lives will be consumed by anger. When vengeance is served, it leaves one empty. Anger is a hard urge to satisfy and can become habitual. But forgiveness allows us to move on.
>
> There is also a more compelling reason to forgive. Forgiveness is a gift – it is mercy. It is a gift that I have received and also given away. In both cases, it has been completely satisfying.

When infamous "pick-ax murderer" Karla Faye Tucker was executed on February 3, 1998, in Huntsville, Texas, small clusters of death penalty protesters held a candle-light vigil. But many more of the hundreds gathered outside the prison were there to cheer her death. A cardboard sign waved by one man said it all: "May heaven help you. It's sure as hell we won't!"

Inside the prison, however, a man named Ron Carlson was praying for Karla – not in the witness room for her victims' families, where he could have been, but in the one set aside for the family of the murderer.

It has been two years since I met Ron and heard his remarkable journey from hatred to reconciliation, but what he told me sticks in my mind as if it were yesterday:

> Shortly after I came home one day at five after a hard day's work – it was the 13th of July, 1983 – the phone rang. It was my father. He said, "Ronnie, you need to come over to the shop right away. We have reason to believe your sister has been murdered." I was floored. I couldn't believe it. I couldn't even believe it when I saw her body being carried out of an apartment on television.
>
> Deborah was my sister, and she raised me. My mother and father divorced when I was very young, and my mother died when I was six. I had no brothers – just one sister – so Deborah was very special. *Very* special.
>
> Deborah made sure I had clothes to wear, and that there was food on the table. She helped me do my homework, and slapped me on the hand when I did something wrong. She became my mother.
>
> Now she was dead, with dozens of puncture wounds all over her body, and the pick-ax that made them had been left in her heart. Deborah was not one to have enemies. She had simply been in the wrong place at the wrong time. The murderers had come over to steal motorcycle parts from the house where she was staying,

and when they discovered Jerry Dean – the guy she was with – they hacked him to death. They were high on drugs. Then they discovered Deborah, so they had to kill her too…

Houston was in an uproar. Headlines screamed the gory details of the crime, and the entire city lived in fear. A few weeks later the murderers – two drug addicts named Karla Faye Tucker and Daniel Ryan Garret – were turned in by relatives. Subsequently tried and convicted, they were both sentenced to death by lethal injection. (Daniel later died in prison.) Still, Ron felt no relief:

> I was glad they were caught, of course, but I wanted to kill them myself. I was filled with sheer hatred, and I wanted to get even. I wanted to bury that pick-ax in Karla's heart, just like she had buried it in my sister's.

Ron says that he was a problem drinker and drug abuser before his sister's death, but that after he buried her, he became more heavily involved than ever. Then, about a year later, his father was shot to death.

> I was often drunk, and I'd get high on LSD, marijuana, whatever I could get my hands on, as often as I could. I also got into a lot of fights with my wife. I was very angry. I even wanted to kill myself…
>
> Then one night, I just couldn't take it any more. I guess I had come to the point where I knew I had to do something about the hatred and rage that was building

in me. It was getting so bad that all I wanted to do was destroy things and kill people. I was heading down the same path as the people who had killed my sister and my dad. Anyway, I opened a Bible, and began to read.

It was really weird. I was high – I was smoking doobies and reading the word of God! But when I got to where they crucified Jesus, I slammed the book shut. For some reason it struck me like it never had before: My God, they even killed Jesus!

Then I got down on my knees – I'd never done this before – and asked God to come into my life and make me into the type of person he wanted me to be, and to be the Lord of my life. That's basically what happened that night.

Later I read more, and a line from the Lord's Prayer – this line that says "forgive us as we forgive" – jumped out at me. The meaning seemed clear: "You won't be forgiven until you forgive. I remember arguing to myself, "I can't do that, I could never do that," and God seemed to answer right back, "Well, Ron, *you* can't. But through me you can."

Not long after that I was talking on the phone with a friend, and he asked me if I knew that Karla was in town, at the Harris County Jail. "You ought to go down there and give her a piece of your mind," he said. Now this friend didn't know where I'd been going spiritually, and I didn't tell him. But I did decide to go see Karla.

When I got there, I walked up to her and told her that I was Deborah's brother. I didn't say anything else at first.

She looked at me and said, "You are *who?*" I repeated myself, and she still stared, like she just couldn't believe what she was hearing. Then she started to cry.

I said, "Karla, whatever comes out of all this, I want you to know that I forgive you, and that I don't hold anything against you." At that point all my hatred and anger was taken away. It was like some great weight had been lifted off my shoulders.

Ron says he talked with Karla at length, and that during their discussion he discovered that she, too, had recently come to believe in God, and that her faith had changed her whole outlook on life. It was then that he decided he would have to return and find out more about her:

> At first I had just wanted to go in, forgive her, and move on, but after that first visit I needed to go back. I wanted to find out if she was really sincere about this Christian walk she claimed to be on. I also wanted to find out why people kill, why they murder each other. I never found that out, but I did find out that Karla was real. I also found out, through her, that people *can* change and that God is real.
>
> Karla's mother had been a prostitute and a drug addict, and she'd introduced her daughter to all that when she was very young. Karla started shooting drugs when she was ten. It was only in prison that she turned her life around – through a ministry at the Harris County Jail that reached out to the women, gave them free Bibles, and helped them find something to live for.

Ron visited Karla on death row every second month or so for the next two years, and he also wrote letters to her. They were soon close friends. He remembers:

> People just couldn't understand it. They said something was obviously wrong with me – that I should hate the person who killed Deborah, not reach out to her. One relative told me I was disgracing my sister's memory, the way I was acting, and that she was probably rolling in her grave. Another made a public statement the day Karla was to be executed about how happy he and his family were to know that she would soon be dead. He said, "We have a saying in Texas – 'What goes around, comes around.'"

Karla herself was mystified by Ron's attitude toward her. Talking with a Dutch television crew who interviewed her shortly before her execution, she said: "It's unbelievable. Amazing. Forgiveness is one thing. But to go beyond that and reach out to me – to actively love me…?" If anything, she found it easier to understand the thousands of Texans who wanted her dead:

> I can understand their rage. Who wouldn't? It's an expression of their hurt and pain. And I know people don't think I deserve forgiveness. But who *does* deserve it? I've been given a new life, and the hope – the promise – that this is not the final reality.

Karla went to her death bravely, smiling as she made her last statement – "I am so sorry…I hope God gives you all peace through this" – and humming as she was strapped to the gurney and pumped with lethal chemicals.

As for Ron, he insists that it was useless to execute her: "It does no good whatsoever to kill anyone. It does not make our streets safer. It just makes more victims. Sure, I miss my sister. But I miss Karla too."

7

When Reconciling Is Impossible

It may be infinitely worse to refuse to forgive than to
murder, because the latter may be an impulse of a moment
of heat, whereas the former is a cold and deliberate choice
of the heart.

GEORGE MACDONALD

When Marietta Jaeger's seven-year-old daughter was kidnapped from their tent during a camping trip in Montana,
her initial reaction was one of rage:

> I was seething with hate, ravaged with a desire for re-
> venge. "Even if Susie were brought back alive and well
> this minute, I could kill that man," I said to my husband,
> and I meant it with every fiber of my being.

Justifiable as her reaction was, Marietta says she soon realized that no amount of anger could bring her daughter
back. Not that she was ready to forgive her daughter's kid-

napper: she told herself that to do that would be to betray her daughter. Yet deep down inside, she sensed that forgiving him was the only way she would ever be able to cope with her loss.

It was that sense – that and sheer desperation – that led her to pray not only for her daughter's safe return, but for her kidnapper as well. As she prayed over weeks, and then months, her prayers became easier and more earnest. She simply had to find the person who had taken away her beloved child. And she even felt an uncanny desire to talk with him face to face.

Then one night, a year to the minute after her daughter had been abducted, Marietta received a phone call. It was the kidnapper. Marietta was afraid – the voice was smug and taunting – but she was also surprised at her strange but genuine feeling of compassion for the man at the other end of the line. And she noticed that, as she calmed down, he did too. They talked for over an hour.

Luckily Marietta was able to record their conversation. Even so it was months before the FBI finally tracked him down and arrested him, and it was only then that she knew her daughter would never come home. The investigators had found the backbone of a small child among the kidnapper's belongings.

State law offered the death penalty, but Marietta was not out for revenge. She writes: "By then, I had finally come to learn that true justice is not about punishment, but restoration and rehabilitation." Later she requested that her child's killer be given an alternative sentence of life imprisonment with psychiatric counseling. The tormented young man soon committed suicide, but she never regretted her decision to offer him help. And her efforts at peacemaking did not end there. Today, she is part of a group that works for reconciliation between murderers and the families of victims.

Kelly, a long-time acquaintance, lost her fiancé when he left her ten days before their wedding date. It was the last time she ever saw him. They had been engaged for more than a year, and although the relationship had occasionally faltered, she was sure that this time everything was going to work out. She was deeply in love, and very excited. She had finally graduated from nursing school, and her wedding dress was nearly finished. Then everything fell apart:

> My fiancé revealed that he had been dishonest with me – there were things in his past that were still an obstacle to our marriage. To make things worse, he wanted to run away from it all rather than confront it. I was shattered. I wept for days and was heartbroken for years. I blamed myself for his dishonesty, and I became bitter.

Thirty years later, Kelly is still single, but she is no longer bitter. Even though she cannot tell him, she has genuinely and entirely forgiven her fiancé. And although she sometimes still aches for the marriage that never was and the love she lost, she has found fulfillment of another kind in helping and serving other people – the old and the sick, expectant mothers, and disabled children. Happy and energetic, she is too busy to entertain self-pity, and few, if any, of her friends know about her past:

> Because I am single, I can do things a busy wife and mother could never do. I can give of myself whenever and wherever I am needed. And I have cared for and loved more children than I ever could have otherwise. But before I could do any of this, I had to stop focusing on myself and my loss. First I had to forgive.

When Julie discovered that her husband, Mike, was molesting their daughter, she was beside herself with shock and anger. Yet after confronting him and taking steps to ensure that his behavior would not continue, she decided to stay with him. For one thing, she wanted to believe him when he insisted it would never happen again; for another, she could not bear the thought of asking him to leave. But the family broke up anyway.

I was foundering on the verge of desperation. Mike had become a stranger to me, and I could no longer live with him in what had become a hell. We stayed together about a year, struggling to rebuild our relationship – or at very least keep it from falling any further apart – but it was no use.

Finally I left Mike and moved back to my old home-town, taking the children with me. I was angry, hurt, hateful, rejected, despairing, outraged, humiliated – and even this long string of adjectives cannot express what I felt. A battle raged in my heart.

Part of me wanted to forgive Mike, but another part wanted to lash out at him in revenge. This was especially so after he divorced me and married again. Every time I thought of his new wife it rekindled my anger.

This was my battle: deep down, I felt I should forgive Mike, and I genuinely wanted to. But how should I express my forgiveness practically? And how could I, when he showed so little remorse?

I didn't want to gloss over what he had done in any way, and I had let him know, when I left him, that I could never allow our children to stay with him again. But aside from that there seemed nothing I could do, other than acknowledge the fact that our marriage was over for good, and accept the divorce.

It has not been an easy battle, and it continues still, as I witness the effect of the abuse and the breakup on our five children. I have also discovered that forgiveness is not a one-time thing – it must be affirmed again and again.

Sometimes I doubt that I have ever forgiven Mike at all, and I have to battle through that, too. But I know that, ultimately, the wrongs he did to me cannot destroy me.

Anne Coleman, the woman whose story I told in the first chapter, came to a similar conclusion after the murder of her daughter, Frances, and the subsequent death of her son, Daniel, who could not cope with his sister's death. Though this double tragedy shattered every semblance of "normal" life for their mother, she was determined to stand strong, and not to concede defeat. Today, instead of nursing her own wounds, she tends to those of the people around her. In fact, she does much more than that in her work as a volunteer counselor to the men on Delaware's death row.

Anne's involvement with prison inmates began after she met Barbara Lewis, a woman whose son had been sentenced to death. After going to see him together, they began to visit other inmates as well:

> That's how I met Billy. He'd had no visitors, and he was very lonely. I cry when I think of how he was hanged; how they made him stand on the gallows in that howling wind for at least fifteen minutes while they waited for the witnesses to arrive. After his execution I thought I couldn't go on.
>
> Then I got to know a little boy called Marcus. His father is also on death row. He has no mother and has lost

both of his sisters, and he has nightmares because now he's going to lose his father, too…

I know that hating someone is not going to bring my daughter back. And at this point, I don't know if I'll ever find the person who killed her, anyway. But one has to find healing somehow, and I've found it by helping the Barbaras and Marcuses of this world. Helping them has given me more healing than I ever imagined.

On April 20, 1999, Brad and Misty Bernall of Littleton, Colorado, lost their daughter Cassie in a school shooting that left her and fourteen other classmates dead. Like Anne, the Bernalls may never fully come to terms with their daughter's death. In a way, that would be unnatural, because the memory of a child is something a parent wants to keep alive forever. Nor are they ready, yet, to say "I forgive" from the bottom of their hearts. Still, they are "working on it," as Misty says, rather than seeking revenge.

Brad and Misty are frustrated by the knowledge that their daughter's killers might have been stopped, had parents, law enforcement officials and school administrators intervened earlier. Nevertheless, while many families of school shooting victims around the country have hired attorneys, filed lawsuits, and become embroiled in bitter shouting matches over who is to blame for their children's deaths, the Bernalls have resisted invitations to join the fray. As Misty put it in a book she wrote about her daughter about six months after her death:

> Anger is a destructive emotion. It eats away at whatever peace you have, and in the end it causes nothing but greater pain than you began with. It also makes it that much harder for others to console you, when you're busy nursing resentment. It's not as if I don't have those seeds in me – I know I do – but I'm not going to let other people water them.
>
> There's also the whole question of revenge. It's normal, I think, to want to bite back, whether through filing a lawsuit or by other means. But in the case of Cassie's murderers, we could never go after their families. Even if we did sue them and won, no amount of money is going to bring our daughter back.

Clearly, not every story has a tidy ending. Sometimes, as happened in Littleton, murderers kill themselves. Sometimes, as in the case of Anne's daughter, they are never caught. Fiancés (and even spouses) up and leave, never to be heard from again. Marietta tried to reach out to the man who kidnapped her daughter, and found him too tormented to be helped. Then there are those like Julie, who gather up their courage and confront the person they want to forgive, only to discover that he is not the least bit sorry for his actions. Anyone whose wounds are left to bleed in such painful ways is bound to remain affected for the rest of his or her life.

Unfortunately, those who take the most pains to demand an apology may find, in the end, that it can never come, and those who smolder year after year, burning with the desire to see justice finally served, may ultimately be disappointed. The fuel of bitterness is always expended in vain. But the opposite is true, too. The love of a forgiving heart is never wasted. It can fill the deepest hole and heal the deepest wound.

8

Forgiving in Everyday Life

To love at all is to be vulnerable. The only place outside
Heaven where you can be perfectly safe from all the dangers
and perturbations of love is Hell.

C. S. LEWIS

Most of us will probably never be faced with forgiving a
murderer or rapist. But all of us are faced daily with the
need to forgive a partner, child, friend or colleague – perhaps dozens of times in a single day. And while doing the
latter may be less difficult than the former, it is just as
important. In his poem "A Poison Tree," William Blake
shows how the smallest resentment can blossom and bear
deadly fruit:

> I was angry with my friend:
> I told my wrath, my wrath did end.
> I was angry with my foe:
> I told it not, my wrath did grow.

And I water'd it in fears,
Night and morning with my tears;
And I sunned it with smiles,
And with soft deceitful wiles.

And it grew both day and night,
Till it bore an apple bright;
And my foe beheld it shine,
And he knew that it was mine,

And into my garden stole
When the night had veil'd the pole:
In the morning glad I see
My foe outstretched beneath the tree.

The seeds of Blake's tree are the petty grudges of everyday life. Often they are so small that they are barely noticeable, at least at first. But even if we do not consciously tend to them, they will germinate over time. That is why it is so important to weed out even the most insignificant ones as soon as they take root in us – before they can grow.

I had to learn not to hold on to grudges early in my life. My childhood was a happy one for the most part, but I had my share of unpleasant experiences. A sickly child, I was diagnosed with hydrocephalus ("water on the brain") soon after I was born, and a doctor told my mother I would never walk. Even though this did not prove to be true – I started walking at two-and-a-half – classmates who found out about my condition began calling me "water head."

Though this probably hurt my parents more than me, the nickname upset me a good deal too.

When I was six, I had to have a large tumor removed from my leg. This was the first of many such operations over the next three decades. The surgery lasted two hours, and the threat of infection – this was before the days of antibiotics, and we lived in the backwoods of Paraguay – hung over me for days. After my leg was stitched shut, I had to walk home from the hospital: no one offered me crutches, let alone a wagon ride. I can still see my father's shocked face as I limped into our house, though he didn't say a thing.

That was typical of my parents. We never heard them speak ill of others, and they did not allow us to, either. Like any other parents, they struggled with their feelings when they felt that one of us children had been mistreated, whether by a teacher or any other adult. But they insisted that the only way to overcome the little indignities of life was to rise above them by forgiving.

When I was fourteen, we moved to the United States. The change from a village in the South American wilderness to a public high school in New York was enormous. The English language was perhaps the biggest barrier for me, but there were other obstacles to fitting in: I felt awkward and clumsy, and on top of that I was naturally shy. In short, I had very little self-esteem.

Every child wants to be recognized by his peers, and I was no different. I desperately wanted to be accepted, and I went out of my way to please my new classmates. At first I was spurned, especially by the class bully. Then I began to fight back, taunting him by talking about him behind his back and laughing in his face when he tried to find out what I had said. Not surprisingly, I received my share of bloody noses.

In my twenties, I dealt with more damaging feelings of rejection, when the woman I was engaged to turned her back on me and broke off our relationship. It was a struggle for me to let go of my hurt feelings and forgive her, especially since I had no idea why she had ended the relationship. Later I convinced myself that it was my fault that things had gone wrong, because I was such an awkward misfit, and I had to forgive myself too.

A few years later, my hopes were dashed again, when another woman broke off our relationship after several months. My world crashed around me as I tried to make sense of what had happened. What had I done wrong?

That second time it took even longer to battle my emotions and rebuild my confidence. But my father assured me that in time I would find the right partner, and a few years down the road he proved to be right.

Perhaps the hardest thing about practicing forgiveness in daily life is that it requires us to confront the reality of our feelings toward those we know best. It is difficult enough to forgive a stranger we might never see again, but it is much harder to forgive a person we love and trust. Our family, our friends, the people we feel closest to at work – they not only know our strengths, but also our weaknesses, our frailties, and our quirks. And when they turn on us, we are often left reeling. At least that's what Clare Stober, a former businesswoman who is now a member of my church, experienced:

> Before leaving the advertising agency I co-owned and moving to another state, I had to settle affairs with my partner of ten years. This was complicated by the fact that he and his wife had once been very close to me and had been fellow church members for the past fifteen years. Over time we had grown apart, and I felt I could no longer continue working with them.
>
> None of our advisors wanted to tell me how best to divide our assets equitably. I wanted to go beyond just being fair – I wanted nothing weighing on my conscience – so I made a proposal to that effect. I thought it was a very generous distribution. But my partner saw the whole thing differently and stopped talking to me the day I told him of my desire to leave the business.

Unfortunately, it was two more months before I felt my tasks were sufficiently handed over, and the transition was long, silent, lonely, and punctuated by angry words.

We still had not signed an agreement by the time I left. Lawyers had been brought in by both sides, but they only clouded the waters. I had wanted an outside source to arbitrate the offer, but my partner fired the arbitrator and sought advice instead from an accountant we had worked with for seven years. The accountant quickly realized that his future lay with the partner who was continuing with the business and helped him to make my leaving very difficult.

It took a lot of offers and counter-offers to come to a final agreement. I won't go into details here, but the result of their demands was that I was made liable for one-half of the firm's earnings for the last full year I was with them, from January to December, even though I only received my share of the earnings through June. I ended up paying $50,000 in taxes which they should have paid.

When I realized what they had done, and that they had done it with forethought and deliberation, I was so angry I could not sleep for days. I felt they had conspired to crush me. I've been through a lot of difficult times in my life, but I have never spent so many sleepless nights, tossing and turning, consumed by anger and deep hurt. When I thought about what had happened during the day, the waves of anger that welled up within me were so powerful they would leave me shaking.

To make matters worse, a friend asked me, "What are you so upset about? It's only money." That made me even more angry. Sure it was "only money," and I didn't really need it at the time. But it was a *lot* of money, and it was mine, and they had cheated me. Obviously, the IRS could not be put off, though, so I wrote the check and hoped in a God of vengeance.

My journey to forgiveness took years. It was like crossing a stream by hopping from one stone to another. I took the first step as I was driving alone one night, listening to the radio, and a song came on about forgiveness. The performer explained the lyrics before he sang it. He talked about how we keep our hurts in a cupboard in our hearts and repeatedly bring them out to turn them over and replay them. We examine our hurts over and over, and nurse our self-pity.

There was a surprise at the end of the song: it talked about how we think we're imprisoning those who have hurt us by not forgiving them, but if we look at the face of the person locked in the tower, we'll see that it is our own. At that point I knew, at least intellectually, that forgiveness was the key to getting on with my life.

I took a second step when I began to examine my own feelings and realized that I was more hurt by my partner's cheating me out of money, than by his slander. It began to bother me that I had let money have such a hold on my life and feelings.

Another step came about a year later when I was embarking on a new chapter of my life in a new location. I was talking with a friend who knew my old partner, and she asked me if I had ever forgiven him. I quickly said, "Sure." She wasn't satisfied, but pressed further, explaining to me how important forgiveness was for both of our futures, even if we no longer worked together. She said that by not forgiving him, I was somehow binding him and not letting him get on with his life – not to mention that I was hurting my own future in the same way. I asked my friend, "So how does forgiveness work, then?" She described it as a gift – we can will to forgive as much as we want, but ultimately it must be given to us. Reluctantly, I began to will myself to forgive – though in retrospect I see that I still felt it was my partner who should be asking for forgiveness, not me.

The final step came later, during a time of deep spiritual introspection. I was trying to clear up everything in my life that had gone wrong up to that point, and make a clean slate before God. Frankly, I was getting nowhere – I thought I had nothing to clear up.

Then it hit me like a ton of bricks. Sure, I had been wronged, but I had done more than an equal share of wrongs in my life – against my partner, and against others. I sat down and wrote him a letter, telling him how much bitterness I had carried, and asking his forgiveness. I felt such a release as I licked that envelope and put the letter in the mail. No matter what their answer, I could now be free of my anger.

About a month later, the same friend who had advised me to forgive happened to call me and asked me if I had been able to do so. I told her that I had, and that I now felt free. She answered, "I thought so. I've noticed a new freedom in him, too."

Already as a teenager, my father was known for his ability to listen and his tendency to think the best of people, and when he became a pastoral counselor, these qualities stood him in good stead. Neither assertive nor articulate (he learned English only as an adult), he would rarely dispense advice, but take in a person's problems quietly and then offer a personal insight or an encouraging word.

Wherever Papa went, people wanted to talk to him. Many had things they wanted to get off their chests; others just needed a receptive ear. Whatever the case, they knew he would make time for them. Unfortunately, the very thing that drew people to him netted him the criticism of envious colleagues, who took advantage of his trust and turned on him.

Papa began to suffer from kidney problems around the time I was born, and as I grew up these problems became worse. Physically, life was harsh in the rural community where we lived: tropical diseases were rampant, and the infant mortality rate was very high. Added to that, there were tensions in our settlement, a close-knit intentional community that consisted primarily of immigrants who had fled wartime Europe.

Given these circumstances, the burden of Papa's responsibilities – he was an appointed leader of the community – weighed on him so heavily that it affected his health. At one point, after several weeks of steady physical decline, his doctors even told him he had only forty hours to live. Fearing the worst, he summoned the entire community to his bedside and passed on his duties to three other men, one of them his brother-in-law.

As it turned out, Papa miraculously recovered, but rather than handing back his responsibilities to him, the community's new leaders told him that his working days were over: the doctor had declared him too weak to continue his demanding schedule.

In fact, the doctor had simply suggested a few weeks of rest. But the "misunderstanding" was deliberate – my father's colleagues wanted him out of the ministry. As ammunition for their case, they reminded him of the emotional instability he had displayed at the height of his illness, when he had seen strange things and had had bizarre dreams. What, they asked him, were they to make of all that? (Thirty years later another doctor discovered the reason for his hallucinations: they were a side-effect of the primitive bromide medications used to treat him.)

Never the kind of person to fight back, Papa meekly gave in and took a new job in the local missionary hospital.

Not long after that, new problems surfaced. Worried that the community was moving away from its original basis – faith, mutual service, and brotherly love – and becoming a committee-led bureaucracy driven by rules and regulations, my parents joined a handful of other members in voicing their concerns. But they were not heard. Instead of welcoming their questions, the leadership accused them of trying to create a split, and several, including Papa, were excommunicated.

Papa was a skilled gardener – he had studied agriculture in Zurich – but even so he was unable to find work. As an outspoken opponent of Nazism, he was looked on with suspicion by the local Germans, who tended to be sympathetic toward Hitler. As for the British and American expatriates in the area, they feared him because he was German. Finally, he found employment as a farm manager in a leper colony.

In the early 1940s there was no cure for leprosy, and Papa was warned that if he accepted the position he might never see his wife or children again (At that time the disease was thought to be contagious). But what could he do? He had to support himself somehow. He took the job.

Finally, after many months, Papa was permitted to rejoin the community. The day he returned I was so excited

I could hardly stand it. As soon as I saw him I jumped into his arms. Then, riding on his shoulders as he walked toward our house, I called out to everyone we passed, "Papa is home!" Amazingly, my joy was met mostly with icy stares. It was only years later that I was able to understand. Yes, Papa had been allowed to come back. But he hadn't been forgiven.

Though the anguish my parents suffered in those years must have affected them both deeply, it never embittered them. In fact, it was only decades later that I found out about all that they had gone through – and not from them, but from friends. When I asked them why they hadn't stood up for themselves, my father said simply, "No matter how many times you are betrayed, it is always better to forgive than to live in a spirit of anger and mistrust." I was deeply impressed by his attitude, but I was also horrified. How would I react, I wondered, if I were treated in such a way?

In 1980 I found out. My church suddenly asked me to step down from my work as assistant elder to my father, a task I had been appointed to almost ten years earlier. To this day I am not completely sure why it happened. Most probably there was an element of the same divisive jealousy that had resulted in my father's expulsion forty years earlier. Whatever the reason, the very same people who had always praised and encouraged me – including several friends, colleagues, and even several close relatives – began to find fault with everything I had ever done.

Confused and angry, I was tempted to fight back. My father was by then senior elder of four large congregations, and he needed me more than ever; only weeks before, my mother had died of cancer. On top of that, I couldn't see what I had done wrong. True, I was known to be blunt about what I felt, especially in matters where I felt that politeness or diplomacy would mask a real issue, and not everyone in our church appreciated this. Still, I had always tried to be humble and considerate. And now this! I desperately wanted to set my record straight and reestablish my "rightful" place.

Papa, however, refused to support me in fighting back. Instead he pointed me to the Sermon on the Mount, where Jesus speaks of forgiving others for their trespasses so that we, too, may be forgiven. He reminded me that in the end we won't have to answer for what others do to us – only for what we do to them.

Suddenly I realized I wasn't as blameless as I had thought I was. I began to see that deep down I held grudges against various members of my church, and that instead of trying to justify myself, I needed to get down on my knees and ask God to forgive me. Then I would find strength to forgive.

I did this, and right away it seemed as if a dam had burst open somewhere deep down inside my heart. Before, my struggle had centered on the pain of hurt pride; now I was able to see things from a new perspective – and it all seemed rather petty.

With a new determination to set things straight and take the blame for whatever tensions existed, I went to everyone I felt I might have hurt in some way in the past, and asked them to forgive me. As I went from one person to the next, the knots in my heart seemed to undo themselves one by one, and by the end of it I felt like a new person.

That year was a very painful one for me, but it was also an important one, because it taught me several lessons I will never forget. First, it does not matter if people misunderstand you or accuse you unjustly. What matters is standing right before God. Second, even though the decision to forgive must always come from within, it is never a matter of willpower alone. The most powerful source of strength is always your own need – your own acknowledgment of weakness and your own experience of being forgiven. Finally, if your forgiveness is going to bear fruit, the soil around it – the soil of the heart – must be soft enough for it to grow in. If it is not soft – if you are not willing to be humble and vulnerable – your forgiveness will never be more than a fruitless gesture.

Humility and vulnerability are not easy virtues to acquire. In my experience, they come only with hard work, practice, patience, and pain. Still, life is poorer without them. As M. Scott Peck writes:

> There is no way that we can live a rich life unless we are willing to suffer repeatedly, experiencing depression and despair, fear and anxiety, grief and sadness, anger and the agony of forgiving, confusion and doubt, criticism and rejection. A life lacking these emotional upheavals will not only be useless to ourselves; it will be useless to others. We cannot heal without being willing to be hurt.

9

Forgiveness and Marriage

People ask me what advice I have for a married couple
struggling in their relationship. I always answer: pray and
forgive. And to young people from violent homes, I say: pray
and forgive. And again, even to the single mother with no
family support: pray and forgive.

MOTHER TERESA

Over many years of marriage counseling, I have seen again
and again that unless a husband and wife forgive each other
daily, marriage can become a living hell. I have also seen
that the thorniest problems can often be resolved with
three simple words: I am sorry.

Asking one's partner for forgiveness is always difficult,
because it requires humility, vulnerability, and the acknowledgment of weakness and failure. Yet there are few
things that make a marriage more healthy.

Dietrich Bonhoeffer, the German pastor imprisoned by Hitler for his opposition to the Nazi regime, used to tell the members of the small community he founded about the need to "live together in forgiveness," because without forgiveness no human fellowship – least of all a marriage – can survive. "Don't insist on your rights," he once wrote. "Don't blame each other, don't judge or condemn each other, don't find fault with each other, but accept each other as you are, and forgive each other every day from the bottom of your hearts."

In thirty-three years of marriage, my wife, Verena, and I have had no lack of opportunities to test our willingness to forgive. Only a week after our wedding we had our first crisis. We had invited my parents and sisters over to dinner in our new apartment, and Verena had spent all afternoon cooking. My sister, an artist, had made us a set of pottery dishes, and I set the table with them.

My family arrived and we sat down to eat. Suddenly both ends of the table collapsed – I had not snapped the hinged extensions properly into place. Food and broken pottery covered the floor, and my wife fled the room in tears. It was hours before she could forgive me and laugh about the disaster, which has since become a family legend.

By the time we had eight children, there were plenty of opportunities for disagreements. Every evening Verena would give the children baths and get them into their pajamas, after which she would have them wait for me on the couch with their favorite picture books. As soon as I came home from work, however, they all wanted to go outdoors again and play with me, so we often ended up romping in the yard. Afterward Verena had to clean up the children all over again, which she did, though not without a little justified grumbling.

Most of our children suffered from asthma, and when they were small they woke us almost nightly with their coughing and wheezing. This, too, became a source of occasional tensions, especially when Verena reminded me that I could get out of bed and help them just as well as she could.

There were arguments over my work as well. As a salesman for our publishing house, I spent countless days on the road. And because my territory covered western New York – Buffalo, Rochester and Syracuse – I was often a good six or eight hours' drive away from home. Later my work took me to Canada, Europe, Africa, and even Australia. I always ended up defending such trips as vitally important, but this did little to soothe Verena, who packed my suitcases and stayed behind with the children.

Then there was the *New York Times*. After a hard day on the road, I couldn't see the harm in stretching out with the paper for a few minutes while the children played around me, and I told my wife so. Only later did I realize that it would have been nice to acknowledge the fact that she, too, had been working all day. At the time, I tended to bristle when she reminded me.

I often think about how our marriage might have turned out if we hadn't learned to forgive each other on a daily basis right from the start. So many couples sleep in the same bed and share the same house but remain miles apart inwardly, because they have built up a wall of resentment between themselves. The bricks in this wall may be very small – a forgotten anniversary, a misunderstanding, a business meeting that took precedence over a long-awaited family outing.

Many marriages could be saved by the simple realization that a spouse will never be perfect. Too often, couples assume that a healthy relationship is one that is free from disagreements. Unable to live up to such an unrealistic expectation, they either bottle up their true feelings about each other, or else give up, disillusioned, and separate on grounds of "incompatibility."

Human imperfection means that we will make mistakes and hurt each other, unknowingly and even knowingly. In my own personal life I have found that the only fail-safe solution is to forgive, seventy times seven if necessary. C. S. Lewis writes:

> To forgive the incessant provocations of daily life – to keep on forgiving the bossy mother-in-law, the bullying

husband, the nagging wife, the selfish daughter, the deceitful son – how can we do it? Only, I think, by remembering where we stand, by meaning our words when we say in our prayers each night, "Forgive our trespasses as we forgive those who trespass against us."

The power of forgiveness is wonderfully illustrated by the story of my wife's parents, Hans and Margrit Meier. Hans was a strong-willed man, and his stubbornness caused more than one period of separation in their marriage.

An ardent anti-militarist, Hans was imprisoned only months after their wedding in 1929 because he refused to join the Swiss army. Shortly after his release, the couple was separated again. She had discovered the Bruderhof (the faith community my grandparents founded) and wanted to join it, whereas he was not interested. Having recently given birth to their first child, Margrit begged Hans to join them, but he would not be easily swayed. It was several months before she convinced him to come.

Thirty years and eleven children later, they separated a third time, again over differences regarding their commitment to the Bruderhof. Hans moved to Buenos Aires, where he remained for the next eleven years. Margrit and most of their children, including Verena, emigrated to the United States.

There were no signs of outward rancor, but there were no signs of healing either. Slowly, a wall of bitterness rose up which threatened to keep them apart forever. When Verena and I married in 1966, Hans did not even attend the wedding.

In 1972 I went to Buenos Aires with Verena's brother, Andreas, in an attempt to forge some kind of reconciliation with Hans, but he wasn't interested – at least not at first. He only wanted to recount his side of the story and let us know, once again, how many times he had been hurt. On the last day of our trip, though, something changed. He announced that he would visit us in the United States. He insisted that he would come for just two weeks, and emphasized the fact that he had a return ticket, but it was a start.

When the visit finally materialized, we were disappointed. Hans simply could not forgive. We made every effort to clear up past misunderstandings and acknowledged our guilt in the events leading up to his long estrangement, but we weren't getting anywhere. Intellectually, Hans knew that the only thing standing between us was his inability to forgive. Yet he could not bring himself to do it.

Then came the turning point. In the middle of a discussion that was going nowhere, my uncle Hans-Hermann, who was dying of lung cancer, summoned all his strength, stood up, came over to Hans, and tapped him on the chest saying, "Hans, the change must happen here!" These words cost a tremendous effort: my uncle was receiving supplemental oxygen through nasal tubes and was barely able to speak at the time.

Hans was completely disarmed. His coldness melted away, and he decided then and there to forgive – and to return to his wife and family. After traveling back to Argentina to wind up his affairs, he moved back in with them for good.

Thankfully, in all their years of separation, Hans and Margrit's bond was never completely broken: Hans never touched another woman, and Margrit prayed daily for her husband's return. Still, it took time for them to rebuild their relationship, and the key was surely their willingness to forgive. In the end, their marriage was fully restored to one of deep love and joy in each other. It lasted till Margrit's death sixteen years later.

The story of my parents-in-law shows that a marriage disrupted by long separation can be healed. But what about one broken by adultery? Is it ever fair to expect a cheated wife or husband to dredge up enough courage to forgive and start over again?

Three years ago I counseled Ed and Carol, a couple whose marriage was in shambles. Even before they were married, Ed had been a problem drinker, and this caused tensions in the house from the very start. Aside from that, however, things went fairly well, and they soon had children: first a boy, and then a girl. To any outsider, it would have seemed the perfect marriage. Inwardly, however, Ed and Carol were drifting further and further apart. Then Ed became involved with a neighbor and began an affair with her.

Ed and Carol joined our church a few years later, and around that time he confessed the affair, first to his wife and then to me. As he admitted later, his conscience gave him no peace, and he couldn't stand the pressure of keeping such a secret while pretending that everything was fine.

Carol was dumbfounded. She had sensed for a long time that something was wrong, but she had never imagined such deception. Seething, she told Ed that their marriage was over, and that she would never forgive him.

Though it wasn't hard to sympathize with Carol's anger, I felt that her initial reaction – "I'll never forgive you" – had less to do with the difficulty of forgiving Ed than with the idea of fairness or justice or "getting back" at him. I am sure that deep down she still wanted nothing more than a healthy relationship with the man she loved – the father of her children. But because of the way he had trampled on her, first with his drinking, and then with his adultery, she could not let go of her indignation. Ed didn't deserve another chance, and right now she wasn't going to give him one…

If anything was clear to me, it was that both Ed and Carol needed time and space to work through their problems on their own. For one thing, they were in no state to stay together, and there could be no quick fix. A new relationship had to be built from the bottom up, and the process would be long and painful. For another, I felt that a temporary separation would give them the objectivity they needed to see each other with new eyes, and might even help them rediscover their original love for each other.

Ed and Carol separated, and for the next months I counseled each of them separately. Ed needed help to see the gravity of his unfaithfulness, which he convinced me he wanted to do, while Carol needed help to see that until she forgave him, the deep wounds he had inflicted on her would never heal. As she herself recognized, her worst fear after learning of Ed's affair had been that he would leave her for good, and she didn't want that to happen, so she would have to make it clear to him that she was willing to take him back.

Later, at Carol's request, they began to communicate by phone calls. Then, as their conversations grew longer and more relaxed, they decided they were ready to try meeting face to face again. Carol still had her ups and downs, but as time went on she found herself wanting to give life with Ed another try – and not just for the sake of the children, who had stayed with her when he had moved out of the house, but for her own sake as well. More important, she admitted that Ed's unfaithfulness had not been solely his fault, and that she too bore a guilt for their estrangement. Meanwhile Ed had stopped drinking and begun to assure Carol in other ways as well that he was going to make their marriage work.

Finally, after ten months, Ed and Carol moved back together. In a special service held to celebrate their new beginning, they publicly forgave each other and reconsecrated their marriage. Then, faces beaming, they exchanged new rings.

In a society like ours, where one out of every two marriages ends in divorce, it is tempting to condemn couples who do not stay together. Naturally no one has a right to do that. But after seeing the healing effects of forgiveness in dozens of marriages, including foundering ones like Ed and Carol's, I find it impossible to suppress the hope that hundreds of thousands more could be saved.

10

Forgiving a Parent

It is freeing to become aware that we do not have to be
victims of our past and can learn new ways of responding.
But there is a step beyond this recognition...It is the step of
forgiveness. Forgiveness is love practiced among people ·
who love poorly. It sets us free without wanting anything
in return.

HENRI J. M. NOUWEN

In a world where countless people have been scarred by
childhood abuse – psychological, physical, or sexual –
it is no wonder that television and radio programs, news-
papers and magazines never tire of the theme, but follow
one lurid story after another, day after day. On talk show
after talk show, survivors pour out their anguish to a curious but ultimately jaded and uncaring public. Yet no
amount of soul-baring seems to bring them the healing
they seek. How and where can they find it?

Obviously, the dynamics of every family, as well as the particulars of each instance of abuse, make it useless to offer generic advice or suggestions. Still, the following stories show that the possibility of reconciling should never be ruled out, even in the case of the cruelest parent. They also show the resilience of the human spirit, even when it has been beaten down, and the hope that springs from the mysterious source of strength we call love, whenever we are willing to draw from it.

Don grew up on an Appalachian farm in an extended family of some forty relatives. All of them shared one house and eked out a living on the same small plot of land. His childhood was brutal: he tells of cousins who tried to hang one another and a grandmother who fired at disobedient children with a shotgun full of rock salt.

When Don was about ten his father found a new job and took his wife and children to Long Island. Once there the family's financial situation improved. But their relationships did not. Soon after the move, Don's mother abandoned her husband and children, who were left at the mercy of their father. He beat them so routinely that they lived in constant fear of him. Don still remembers the sick feeling that returned to his stomach each afternoon as he got off the school bus and thought about what the evening might bring.

Then one day Don's father was seriously injured in a collision that left him paralyzed from the neck down. Once the tyrant of the household, he was now a quadriplegic, utterly dependent on others to care for his daily needs.

Most people from such a home would escape as soon as possible, but not Don. With every reason in the world to abandon his father, he remained at his side for years, feeding him and washing, dressing, and exercising the lifeless limbs that had once beat him mercilessly, sometimes to the point of unconsciousness. (Now married, Don has arranged for a hired nurse to provide his father with 24-hour care, but he still lives nearby and visits him frequently.)

Pressed for an explanation, Don has little to say. He never saw his decision to stay on at home as a heroic or sacrificial deed. He never really even thought about it. But what was the option? How could he leave home, when the man who had brought him into the world – his own father – was as helpless as a baby and there was no one to care for him? "Dad needed me, so I stayed."

Bad memories of the past still haunt Don on occasion, and he says his father still has his demons to fight. Life isn't all roses, by any means. But at least they can talk and share the burdens of the emotional battles they have to wage. And in caring for his father Don says he has finally found a measure of the happiness he yearned for as a child. "Call it forgiveness if you like," he says. Whatever it is, it has brought him wholeness and a sense of healing.

Karl Keiderling, a family friend who died several years ago in his eighties, suffered a similarly harsh childhood. The only son of a German working-class family, his early years were clouded by the First World War and the economic devastation that followed it. His mother died when he was four, and his stepmother when he was fourteen. To make matters worse, his father saw him as a burden on the family. When, after his stepmother's death, his father put out an ad in the hopes of finding a new mother for his children, he intentionally excluded Karl: "Widower with three daughters looking for a housekeeper; possibility of future marriage."

Several women applied, and in the end one decided to stay. It was only afterwards that she found out about the existence of a boy in the house, which she never quite got over. Karl's food was always poorer than the rest of the family's, and she complained about him day in and day out.

Karl's father, for his part, was silent in the face of his new wife, and did nothing to defend his son. In fact, he joined her in mistreating the boy and often beat him. His instrument of choice was a leather strap mounted with brass rings. Karl tried to protect himself on occasion, but that only infuriated his father and earned him extra blows to his head and face.

Unlike Don, Karl left home as soon as he could. Attracted by the youth movement sweeping Europe in those years, he joined ranks with a group of young blue-collar socialists who were set on changing the world. Eventually his wanderings brought him to the Bruderhof (at that time still a fledgling commune), where my grandfather welcomed him with an embrace and said, "We've been waiting for you to arrive."

Karl immediately felt at home and decided to stay. He threw himself vigorously into the work, chopping wood, hauling water, and tending the garden. But the agony of his childhood, as well as his feelings of resentment toward his father and stepmother, didn't leave him. Day after day his bitterness grew, hanging around him like a heavy cloud and threatening to block out everything good.

Finally Karl went to my grandfather and poured out his need. The response he got astounded him: "Write to your parents and ask their forgiveness for every instance in which you might have hurt their feelings or otherwise caused them grief. And look only at your own guilt, not theirs." Karl was taken aback, so much so that it took him some time before he felt ready to write. But eventually he did, and amazingly, his father answered the letter.

He never apologized for the way he had beaten Karl as a boy, or acknowledged any guilt of his own. But Karl said it no longer mattered. Through forgiving, he himself had found freedom from the anger that had weighed on him, and a deep sense of peace. Karl never complained about his childhood again.

Maria, a relative from my wife's side of the family, overcame her resentment toward her abusive father in a similar way:

> My mother died at the age of forty-two, leaving behind my father and eight children, aged one to nineteen. Mother's death was devastating for the whole family, but especially for my father, and he suffered an emotional breakdown just when we needed him most. One of the results of his instability was a lack of self-control, and he tried to molest my sister and me. I began to avoid him, and then to hate him.
>
> Soon after this my father moved away, and I left South America for school in Germany. I didn't see him for another seven years. But I held on to my hatred, and it grew inside me.
>
> Later I returned from Europe and became engaged to a childhood friend. My father asked me if we could meet. I flatly refused. I had no desire to see him.

When my fiancé found out about it, however, he did not understand how I could refuse such a meeting. If my father had expressed a longing for reconciliation, wasn't it my duty to respond? It cost me quite a battle to come around to my fiancé's point of view, but he was insistent, and in the end I agreed.

We met my father in a café, found a table, and sat down. Before I had a chance to say a word, he turned to me, broken, and asked for my forgiveness. Disarmed, I melted and assured him of my forgiveness on the spot. There was no way I could have withheld it.

Despite the apparent ease with which Don and Maria forgave their fathers, child abuse is probably the most difficult thing in the world to recover from. Given the imbalance of power between the adult (the perpetrator) and the child (the victim), the blame is always one-sided. And why should the innocent forgive the guilty?

Tragically, many victims of child abuse mistakenly believe that they share some of the blame. They worry that somehow they must have brought on or even deserved what was done to them. In fact, much of the power an abuser holds over his victim, even after the physical abuse itself has stopped, comes from this misguided notion of complicity. It is part of the victimization.

To make matters worse, some people claim that when a victim forgives an abuser, he is implying that he – the victim – is at least partly to blame. Nothing, of course, could be further from the truth. Forgiveness is necessary simply because both victim and victimizer – who in most cases know one another (or are even related) – are prisoners of a shared darkness in which both will remain bound until someone opens the door. Forgiveness is the only way out, and even if an abuser chooses to remain in the darkness, that should not hold the victim back.

Kate, a neighbor in her fifties, was abused by her alcoholic mother for years but is now reconciled to her. Like others, her journey shows that when a victim is changed by the willingness to forgive, her abuser may be affected and transformed as well.

I was born in a small Canadian town shortly after World War II, the eldest of five children. Father's construction job was twenty-five miles away, and between travel and a twelve-hour workday he spent very little time at home.

Money was always a problem, and there were other tensions in our family, though I couldn't explain them. All I knew was that the older I got, the more things seemed to go downhill, especially after the birth of my youngest brother, when I was nine. In retrospect it's very clear what happened: Mother had started drinking.

After Kate's mother began to come home drunk, her parents separated. There was no family life to speak of; the house was neglected, and the laundry was never washed. Everything depended on thirteen-year-old Kate.

By the time Jamie, the youngest, started school, Mother was almost never at home. I never managed to do any homework and was not learning very much. I completely failed ninth grade and had to repeat it the following year.

Later two of my sisters left home, found jobs, and rented an apartment in town. But I stayed. Somebody had to look after the little ones. And as poorly as I did it, at least they were given something to eat.

Then Mother found out about a new source of additional income: in an effort to relieve overcrowding at the local hospital for the mentally and physically disabled, the government was paying people to put up "surplus" patients in their own homes. Mother took in two older men and a woman.

I had to give up my bed to one of the men and share a double bed with the woman, who rarely slept. When I told Mother that I couldn't cope with this and wanted the hospital to take the woman back, she wouldn't hear of it. After all, there was a check coming in every month.

Mother said she'd come home in the evenings to help me, and for a while she did. But the drunken state she came home in! Then she'd say that if it wasn't for me, she wouldn't be in such a mess. At first I didn't understand what she meant, but later I found out: my parents had been forced to marry because my mother was already carrying me.

At times Mother became physically abusive. Then in the morning, if she asked me about the bruises on my face and I told her that she had done it, she claimed I was lying.

At sixteen, Kate quit school in order to devote herself totally to the care of her siblings. Around that time she met her husband, Tom, whom she married two years later. She still remembers the guilt she felt when her mother asked accusingly, "Who is going to do the work around here?" Nonetheless, she moved out of the house, and soon she and Tom were raising a family of their own.

At this point I just wanted to forget about my mother. I had my own little family, and I had Tom's parents, who loved my children. Then, suddenly my mother wanted to reestablish contact. I refused. I finally had some leverage, and I was going to pay her back.

By this time my parents' divorce was finalized, and Mother had stopped drinking. Remarkably enough she had come to realize that the combination of alcohol and blood-pressure medications she was taking would kill her. All the same, I had no desire to visit her. I simply could not trust her.

A few years later, after the birth of another child, Kate found out that her husband had taken a call from her mother, who had asked to come visit the family. Tom had told her she was welcome.

> I was hopping mad. I told Tom, "You call her right back and tell her she can't come. Tell her whatever you want to tell her. This is *my* baby, and I'm not willing to share it with her." I was very nasty. Later, however, I began to feel bad, and I went to talk to our pastor. I thought maybe he would have a solution.
>
> As I explained my dilemma to him, he sat there and listened to me. I finished, but he didn't say anything. I waited. I felt fully justified in having done what I did, but I wanted his assurance. I didn't get it. All he said was, "You have to come to peace with your mother."
>
> I said, "You don't know my mother."
>
> He replied, "That has nothing to do with it."
>
> Meanwhile my mother came anyway. She was not well when she arrived, and she needed a lot of care. I did not make it easy for her.
>
> Then, during the last few days of her visit, I sensed that there was something she was trying to tell me. She even seemed willing to listen to what I had to say to her. As we talked, I realized that Mother wanted a new relationship (by then I desperately wanted one, too) and that she was determined to remove whatever was in the way. It was then that I knew I had to forgive her, so I did.

Immediately a wave of relief and healing came over me. It was indescribable, and it has stayed with me to this day.

Not all instances of parent-child estrangement are so black and white. Susan, a Californian from very different circumstances, never suffered real abuse at the hands of her parents. Still she was embittered for years by her mother's personality, which she felt to be distant and cold. And like Kate, she found that the only route to mutual healing was to face her own lack of love and declare a willingness to forgive.

> Ever since I can remember, I have had a difficult relationship with my mother. I feared her angry outbursts, her biting, sarcastic tongue, and I never felt able to please her. As a consequence, I began to nurse a deep anger toward her – a smoldering, hidden anger that made me close myself off to her. I nursed memories of injustices from early childhood, of sharp words and a few blows (none worth remembering). I became extremely sensitive to her reproofs and easily felt rejected.
>
> Somehow we just never had an open, trusting relationship. Instead I looked to the other adults in my life, especially my teachers. My mother resented my attachment to them but was never able to express it. I can remember wishing to be taken out of my family, to be adopted by one of them. I can also remember a strong physical

feeling of not belonging that would come over me in waves. But in my desire to be accepted, I tried to be "good" and hid my true feelings.

Things only became worse as I grew into adolescence. I found more and more ways to subtly act out my anger and do what I wanted to do. I also found more ways to sneak around my mother. I even "got back" at her by having a secret affair with our parish priest, who often socialized with my parents.

That relationship eventually ended, and I went off to college and a place of my own. Then I married. Still, I continued to be at odds with my mother. It was actually a very strange relationship, because I still desperately wanted to please her.

Mom went through extended periods of physical and emotional crisis over those years, but I found it difficult to sympathize or even show much interest. I finally reached out to her when she was going through a twelve-step program for alcoholics. We had a wonderful week of talking and sharing, but then suddenly the doors closed again. I blamed it on her, though I cannot now say why.

Finally it became clear to me that her strong, self-confident, in-control exterior was just a shell for a very insecure person underneath, and that she was nursing plenty of hurts from her own childhood. We were both trying to reach out to one another in our own way, but both of us were so afraid of rejection that we couldn't be honest with each other. Our efforts were superficial at best.

The breakthrough came a few years later when I was hounded by a friend to listen to a tape of a talk by some writer called Charles Stanley. I had never heard of him, but I was looking for answers to several big questions at the time, so I listened – guardedly. I can't remember exactly what he said, but it was something about relationships, and it was just what I needed to hear at the time. It helped me to see that insofar as my mother and I were estranged, we each had a share of guilt, and until one of us asked the other for forgiveness, the rift might never be breached.

Not long after that I visited my parents. When I was alone with my mother, I asked her to forgive me for the way I had treated her in the past and told her I forgave her too. I admitted that I had been angry at her all of my life, even though I wasn't sure why. She didn't understand why I should be angry, but she too apologized for the hurt she had caused. She said, "What has happened has happened, and we can't change that. But we can move on."

For anyone who feels trapped in the quagmire of a difficult relationship, these words are as vital as they are simple. No one can undo the past. But each of us can choose to forgive, and each of us can move on.

11

Blaming God

> It is not right to try to remove all suffering, nor is it right
> to endure it stoically. Suffering can be used, turned to good
> account. What makes a life happy or unhappy is not out-
> ward circumstances, but our inner attitude to them.
>
> EBERHARD ARNOLD

In most cases, when the subject of forgiving comes up,
we think of it in terms of our willingness (or unwilling-
ness) to stop blaming a person who has hurt us. Sometimes, though, an injury has no human cause, and try as
we might, we cannot find anyone who is truly at fault.

To those who have no belief in God, the result may be
a sense of undirected annoyance at the hand dealt them
by life. To those who believe, the result is often anger at
God. Frustrated by our inability to pin down a reason for
our pain, which we are quick to see as unjustified and
undeserved, we rebel against it and accuse God. "How can

a merciful God permit *this?*" In the end, our frustration may turn to resentment, or even to rage.

In many ways, it is easier (even for someone who doesn't actually believe in a higher power) to blame God than to face the possibility that there really might be no one to blame. Anger is a legitimate stage of grief, even when there's no obvious target for us to direct it at. It needs to be expressed and dealt with if we hope to find healing and move on.

Still, it is fruitless to stay angry at God. We can hold him responsible for hurting us, but he cannot very well apologize. If there is anything to be done about circumstances we wish we could change, but can't, it is to accept them gracefully. In doing so we may find that even the greatest obstacle can become an opportunity for growth.

Whenever I am tempted to blame God, I remember a period of great frustration I went through several years ago, and what I learned from it. It all began on the way home from a fishing trip in upstate New York – a welcome chance to escape the pressures of my work for a few days – when I noticed that I was losing my voice. At first I ignored it, expecting it to improve within several days. But it only grew worse. Finally my doctor referred me to a specialist. The diagnosis: a paralyzed vocal chord.

The specialist reassured me that my voice would eventually recover, but weeks and then months went by, and there was no change. His prescription was complete voice rest (I wasn't even allowed to whisper) and frustrating as it was, I held to it religiously. Still there was no improvement. I wondered if I would ever speak again.

To make things worse, right during this time my congregation became embroiled in an extended crisis involving a fallout between several longstanding members. At meeting after meeting I was asked for my input as senior pastor, but instead of being able to respond, I could only sit by in silence and write down the things I most wanted to say.

When a capability like speech – or anything else we take for granted – is taken away from us, we can choose to see it with new appreciation, as the gift it is. But I was too anxious and upset to do that. To be honest, I was angry. Even if God was testing me, I said to myself, he couldn't have picked a worse time.

It was only with time that I was able to see the whole annoying predicament from another angle: I began to realize that it was providing me with an important chance to develop a more flexible outlook on life, to take myself less seriously, and to make the best of an imperfect situation. Three months later, my voice began to return; now, seven years later, it is back to normal. But I have never forgotten those twelve weeks.

Andrea, a woman in my church, struggled to accept a much heavier burden: she miscarried three times before having a healthy child. Unlike mine, Andrea's story is not, strictly speaking, about blaming or "forgiving" God. For her the battle was to accept the loss of her babies without succumbing to the fear that God was somehow trying to punish her. But in showing how she was able to wrestle through her emotions and find peace, it illustrates a similar theme.

> Neil and I were delighted to find that I was pregnant after only six months of marriage. But one night, just before Christmas, I felt intense pain that grew rapidly worse. Our doctor wanted to send me to the hospital, and our neighbor, a nurse, came to stay with me until we left for town. She confirmed my worst fears – I would probably lose my baby. The emotional pain was at least as severe as the physical. Why, God? Why me? Why do you have to take away this tiny soul so soon? What have I done wrong?
>
> In order to save my life, an operation was necessary. The baby was lost, and I spent weeks recuperating. What a different Christmas this had become!
>
> We agonized over our loss and felt alone in our pain. When one of our relatives said to us, "Cheer up! Maybe you'll have better luck next time," I felt like I had been slapped in the face. Luck? We had just lost a baby, a real person, a child!

Someone sent me a card that said, "The Lord giveth, and the Lord taketh away, blessed be the name of the Lord." That made me really upset. How could I thank God for this horrible, painful experience? I couldn't. And I couldn't stop thinking that somehow God was punishing me, even though I couldn't understand why.

Our pastor consoled me: God is a God of love, not of punishment, and he is there to ease our pain. I grasped at his words as a drowning person grabs onto a pole held out from the shore. Neil's loving support seemed like a visible sign of this love, and we discovered that our pain united us in a new way. The words "Weeping shall endure for the night, but joy comes in the morning" especially comforted me, even when I couldn't feel that joy coming, when it seemed that dawn would never break.

Slowly, with time and with the loving help of those around me, I was able to feel that this deeply painful experience had given me an inkling of the love of God, who cares about the suffering of people and who was, I am convinced, right there beside me in my pain. God became more real to me, and I began to trust his love.

But then, some months later, when I was expecting another baby and hoping fervently that all would go well, the same thing happened again. Severe pain, an emergency trip to the hospital, and an operation to save my life. Again another precious little person lost just after it had come into being. Deep pain tore my heart apart. I wrote in my diary: "I cannot see why; perhaps I never will. I need the assurance of faith – Help me!"

Neil stood faithfully beside me. He had lost a sister to cancer some years before, and what he had written then was a great source of sustenance: "We are separated from God only in physical distance, and that distance is perhaps not great." I hung on to that with all my strength.

Slowly, over weeks and months, the pain of loss lessened, although it has never departed entirely. About a year later I again lost an unborn child. Once more there was deep pain in my heart, but this time no desperation over why.

Today Andrea is the mother of a beautiful six-year-old daughter. Although thinking about her first three pregnancies always brings back a flood of emotions, she is not bitter. In fact, she is even able to point to two good fruits of her anguish: a greater love for her husband, who "went to hell and back with me," and endless gratitude for her only child.

Like Andrea, Jon and Gretchen Rhoads – a young couple in a nearby community – eagerly awaited the birth of their first child. Alan was born after a seemingly normal pregnancy, and in the beginning everything seemed all right. After he was discharged from the hospital, though, his parents noticed something was wrong. Very wrong. Alan didn't eat well. His muscle tone was poor. He lay very still, almost without moving, and when he breathed, he occasionally made strange gurgling sounds.

Alan was quickly admitted to a nearby university hospital, but he was three months old before his problems became clear: he would probably never walk or talk; he was blind; and he had significant abnormalities of the hips, brain, ears, and stomach.

Jon and Gretchen were devastated. They had long suspected that something was wrong, but they hadn't expected it to be this bad. Right away they began to accuse themselves, and it wasn't long before they began to accuse God: Why us?

Jon says that though he was angry, he could never really say at whom. Himself? Gretchen? Alan's doctors? God? Yes, perhaps God, but he couldn't explain why. Still, he refused to become bitter, but concluded instead that "either God does not love us, or this is just how Alan is meant to be. We may never know why, but if we are resentful about Alan's condition, we will kill any joy we have had in him."

Both Jon and Gretchen admit that acceptance is easier to talk about, than to actually practice. There have been plenty of times when they wanted to run away from it all, when they simply couldn't face another visitor offering meaningless words of sympathy.

And while some days bring progress and new hope, others bring setbacks and trials. In his first year alone Alan had a tracheotomy and numerous other surgeries, including an appendectomy. How much more suffering will he have to endure?

In a world quick to offer "early diagnosis" and abortion as the answer to imperfect babies, Alan's parents refuse to see their child as a burden. "He has a great deal to tell us," Gretchen wrote when he was almost one, "and we are not about to let him go."

> His small hand reaches up through a tangle of wires to find my cheek. As I stoop to lift him from his bed, his eyelids lift slightly and he gives me a sleepy grin…In the eleven months since his birth, Alan has been hospitalized five times; we have long since stopped counting the outpatient appointments. Each time we come home with more questions and fewer answers; more tears, and less certainty. But as he snuggles against me and looks around curiously, he grins. His smile is a balm to my heart.
>
> How much more pain can Alan bear? What new hurdles await us? His tracheostomy has taken away the few small adventures we had looked forward to: bottles and the chance to explore solid food. No more gurgles of joy, either, and no more cries of frustration.
>
> If he lives, the doctor tells us, he may outgrow the need for these tubes. If he lives. The words cut me to my heart, and yet his smile continues to give me hope. He is teaching me acceptance every day.

In the end, it is this acceptance Gretchen writes of that allows us to "forgive" God. Without it, we are left rebelling against our lot in life, and fighting every cross we feel unjustly forced to bear. With it, we gain the ability to see our hardships in relation to the suffering of others, and strength to carry them.

12

Forgiving Ourselves

Without being forgiven, released from the consequences
of what we have done, our capacity to act would, as it were,
be confined to a single deed from which we could never
recover; we would remain the victims of its consequences
forever, not unlike the sorcerer's apprentice who lacked the
magic formula to break the spell.

HANNAH ARENDT

When we assure a person who has hurt us that we no
longer hold anything against him, all he has to do is accept our kindness – at least that is what we might hope.
But that is often more easily said than done. For many
people, the problem of guilt cannot be solved with another's forgiveness, or by any external means at all. For
them, peace of mind comes only when they are able to
forgive themselves.

I first met Delf Fransham in 1953. That was the year he moved from the United States to the remote South American village where I grew up and began to teach at the local school. There were eleven of us in his class, all boys, and all ruffians, and a few days into his first term we decided to put him to the test.

One typical Paraguayan morning (humid and around 110 degrees), we offered to take him on a hike. Officially, we wanted to show him the sights. Privately, we wanted to see what he was made of. After leading him at least ten kilometers through jungle, prairie, and swampland, we finally turned back. Shortly after we arrived home he collapsed with heat stroke.

Delf was in bed for days, but we hardly gave it a thought. We had achieved exactly what we wanted – proved him a sissy. But we were in for a small surprise. The day he came back to school he said, "Boys, let's try that hike again." We couldn't believe it! We covered the same route again and, sure enough, this time he did not succumb to the heat. Delf won our respect and our hearts that day, and we trusted him from then on. (There was something else to it, too: a talented athlete, he taught us soccer and loved to play with us.)

Decades later, and only by chance, I found out why Delf had poured so much love and energy into reaching his students. He had lost a child of his own.

Nicholas was born when the Franshams were still living in the United States, and one day as Delf was backing a truckload of firewood into their driveway, two-year-old Nicholas, who was playing outdoors, ran to meet his father. Delf did not see him until it was too late, and ran over him.

Katie, Delf's wife, was busy inside the house when he carried in their little boy, limp in his arms. She remembers:

> I was beside myself – absolutely frantic – but Delf steadied me. We took Nicholas to our doctor, who was also the coroner, and explained what had happened…
>
> There was never any question about forgiving my husband, as I knew I was just as much to blame. Likewise he did not blame me, only himself. We stood in our sorrow together.

Delf, however, could not forgive himself, and the accident haunted him for years. From then on, he went out of his way to make time for children – time he could not spend with the son he had killed.

Looking back, I remember how his eyes often glistened with tears, and wonder what it was that made them come. Was it that he saw his son in us? Was he imagining the boy his toddler would never become? Whatever the reason, it seems that Delf's determination to show love to others was his way of making up for the anguish he had caused himself and his family by unintentionally taking a life. I am convinced that it saved him from brooding, and from nursing his feelings of guilt. Through loving others he was able to forgive himself and regain a sense of wholeness and peace.

John Plummer lives the quiet life of a Methodist pastor in a sleepy Virginia town these days, but things weren't always so. A helicopter pilot during the Vietnam War, he helped organize a napalm raid on the village of Trang Bang in 1972 – a bombing immortalized by the prize-winning photograph of one of its victims, Phan Thi Kim Phuc.

For the next twenty-four years, John was haunted by the photograph – an image that for many people captured the essence of the war: a naked and burned nine-year-old running toward the camera, with plumes of black smoke billowing in the sky behind her.

For twenty-four years John's conscience tormented him. He badly wanted to find the girl to tell her that he was sorry – but he could not. Turning in on himself, he grew more and more depressed (the collapse of two marriages didn't help), and he began to drink.

Then, in an almost unbelievable coincidence, John met Kim during an event at the Vietnam War Memorial on Veterans Day, 1996. Kim had come to Washington, D.C., to lay a wreath for peace; John had come with a group of former pilots unable to come to terms with their shared past, but determined to stick together anyway.

In a speech to the crowd, Kim introduced herself as the girl in the famous photograph. She still suffered immensely from her burns, she said, but she was not bitter, and she wanted people to know that others had suffered even more than she had: "Behind that picture of me, thousands and thousands of people...died. They lost parts of their bodies. Their whole lives were destroyed, and nobody took their picture."

Kim went on to say that although she could not change the past, she had forgiven the men who had bombed her village, and that she felt a calling to promote peace by fostering goodwill between America and Vietnam. John, beside himself, pushed through the crowds and managed to catch her attention before she was whisked away by a police escort. He identified himself as a former pilot in Vietnam and said that he felt responsible for the bombing of her village twenty-four years before. He says:

> Kim saw my grief, my pain, my sorrow...She held out her arms to me and embraced me. All I could say was "I'm sorry; I'm sorry" – over and over again. And at the same time she was saying, "It's all right, I forgive you."

John says that it was vital for him to meet face to face with Kim, and to tell her that he had agonized for years over her injuries. Without having had the chance to get that off his chest, he is not sure he could have ever forgiven himself. As it turned out, of course, he got even more than he hoped for: Kim forgave him.

Reflecting on the way the incident changed his life, John maintains that forgiveness is "neither earned nor even deserved, but a gift." It is also a mystery. He still can't quite grasp how a short conversation could wipe away a twenty-four-year nightmare.

Pat, another Vietnam veteran, is a gentle, quiet man who loves children and horses. In the seven years since I first met him, however, I have become aware that he has a darker side – one that centers on his inability to forgive himself:

Death is on my mind a lot. The deaths I have caused – and wanting my own death – are with me every day. I joke around a lot with the people I work with. I have to, to hide the pain and to keep my mind from thinking. I need to laugh. Laughing keeps the blues away.

But I cannot love. Part of my soul is missing, and it seems I won't ever get it back. I don't know if I can ever forgive myself for all of my wrongs. I live day to day, but I am tired all the time – tired. Will it ever end? I don't see how. It's been with me over twenty-five years now.

People like Pat are often urged to receive formal counseling, to join a support group, or to attend group therapy meetings so as to compare notes with others who have had similar experiences. He has done all of this, and still not found peace. Perhaps, like John, he wishes he could meet the families of those he killed – an unlikely opportunity – or bring the victims themselves back to life so he could ask their forgiveness – an obviously impossible one. So what should he do?

A conversation Robert Coles once had with the psychoanalyst Anna Freud may hint at an answer. Discussing an elderly client with a long and troubled psychological history, Freud suddenly concluded:

> You know, before we say good-bye to this lady, we should wonder among ourselves not only what to think – we do that all the time! – but what in the world we would want for her. Oh, I don't mean psychotherapy; she's had lots of that. It would take more years, I suspect, of psychoanalysis than the good Lord has given her…No, she's had her fill of "us," even if she doesn't know it…This poor old lady doesn't need us at all…What she needs…is forgiveness. She needs to make peace with her soul, not talk about her mind. There must be a God, somewhere, to help her, to hear her, to heal her…and we certainly aren't the ones who will be of assistance to her in that regard!

Freud's point is a valid one, even for a person who claims to have no belief in God. At some level, all of us must come to terms with the parts of ourselves that we wish we could erase. All of us yearn for the freedom to live without guilt. At some level, every one of us longs for forgiveness.

Yet when all is said and done, we cannot acquire it. Sometimes the person we have wronged is unable or unwilling to forgive us. Sometimes we are unable or unwilling to forgive ourselves. Even the best psychoanalysis, the most earnest confession of guilt, may not be enough to assure us of lasting relief or healing.

But the power of forgiveness still exists, and as John Plummer found out, it can work wonders even when we are sure that we have neither earned nor deserved it. It comes to us as a gift, often when we feel least worthy of receiving it. Finally, like any gift, it can be accepted or rejected. What we do with it is up to us.

13

Accepting Responsibility

In the confession of concrete sins the old man dies a painful, shameful death before the eyes of a brother. Because this humiliation is so hard, we continually scheme to avoid it. Yet in the deep mental and physical pain of humiliation before a brother we experience our rescue and salvation.

DIETRICH BONHOEFFER

No one who has read this far will deny that forgiveness can bring about healing, even where healing seemed impossible. Its power might be mysterious, but it is clearly there, and it is so strong that people are sometimes swept away by it against their more rational instincts. All the same it is dangerous to become glib about forgiveness – to act as if it could be plucked off the nearest tree.

Certainly forgiveness is sometimes given and received lightly, or used to whitewash the ugly underside of life. But such forgiveness has no staying power. Even the most genuine declaration of forgiveness will wear thin if it is not accompanied by a change of heart, both in the forgiver and the forgiven. In other words, it must cost something if it is to have any lasting effect.

There is, moreover, little value in seeking forgiveness if we let it touch us only momentarily and then slide back into the same behavior that required an apology in the first place. It is true that forgiveness is a gift and that it comes with no strings attached. But it is a useless one unless we let it change us for the better.

Mark and Debbie, friends of mine who used to be part of a small house church on the West Coast, experienced this hard reality firsthand:

> Over the years we witnessed the disastrous results of ignoring wrongdoing or secretly hiding it. We lived in a small urban community with several people, one of whom was a single man who had fallen in love with a married woman in our group. Some of us tried to tackle their affair by talking with them separately about it. Yet no one dared to bring it out in the open.
>
> Afraid of being judgmental, we chose to believe that this wasn't a very serious matter, at least not serious enough to bring it out into the open. Didn't we all make mistakes? Who were we to judge? We convinced ourselves that confrontation would not only add to their sense of shame and self-condemnation, but also perpetu-

ate the cycle of failure. In the end we tried to forgive their shortcomings and avoided talking about them any further. Now we see that this so-called compassion only perpetuated the problem…The man eventually left, and two years later, the woman he was involved with divorced her husband and followed him.

Far from being unique, incidents like this one are widespread. On the surface they may seem to have little to do with forgiveness, because there is never even a clear recognition of wrongdoing, and therefore no admission of the need for redemption. But at root they have everything to do with it. If, as in the case described above, the problem had been confronted, who knows how different the outcome might have been?

Obvious as it sounds, it is vital to remember that we cannot truly receive forgiveness until we acknowledge our need for it by admitting our wrongdoings to someone else, whether to the person we have hurt or (where that is not possible) to someone we trust. Some people dismiss this practice as "confession" – something for old-fashioned Catholics. Others admit that it can be helpful, but claim that guilt can be taken care of just as easily by recognizing a misdeed and resolving not to repeat it. But that is utter foolishness: it is precisely such a recognition that brings about guilty feelings to begin with. That is why Tolstoy writes that the peace of heart attained by forgiving oneself in such a manner is nothing but "deadness of the soul." It is nothing like the real peace that comes to those who are humble and honest enough to ask those they have wronged for forgiveness.

Guilt works in secret, and it loses its power only when it is allowed out into the open. Often our desire to appear righteous keeps us from admitting our wrongs. Why reveal a foolish choice or a dumb mistake? Yet the more we try to push such things to the back of our minds, the more they will plague us, even if subconsciously. Eventually guilt will add to guilt, and we will become cramped and weighed down.

As for the freedom that comes from owning up to one's faults, Steve, an old friend of mine, says:

> In my search for inner peace I pursued various religions and studied psychology but never received more than partial answers. It was only after I saw my personal life for the shambles it was that I could see how urgently I needed to change, and how much I needed forgiveness.
>
> The pivotal experience came inexplicably and unexpectedly: I was suddenly aware what an enormous avalanche of wrongs I had left behind me. Before, this reality had been masked by pride and by my wanting to

look good in front of others. But now, memories of everything I had ever done wrong poured out of me like a river of bile.

All I wanted was to be free, to have nothing dark and ugly and hidden within me; I wanted to make good, wherever I could, the wrongs I had done. I had no excuses for myself – youth, circumstances, or bad peers. I was responsible for what I had done.

On one page after another I poured it all out in clear detail. I felt as though an angel of repentance was slashing at my heart with his sword, such was the pain. I wrote dozens of letters to people and organizations I had cheated, stolen from, and lied to. Finally I felt truly free.

In *The Brothers Karamazov* Dostoevsky writes about a character who, after confessing to a murder he has kept hidden for decades, experiences the same freedom: "I feel joy and peace for the first time after so many years. There is heaven in my heart…" For the real-life murderer, "heaven" may not come so easily. Still, it should never be ruled out.

Several years ago I began to correspond with Michael Ross, a Cornell graduate turned serial rapist and killer. Given the enormity of his crimes, the terror of his victims in their last minutes, and the grief of their families, the contempt with which most people treat Michael is hardly surprising. To do anything but hate him, they feel, would be to belittle the immense suffering he has caused.

But what about Michael's own suffering? (After my first visit with him, as I embraced him and said goodbye, he broke down and wept. No one had hugged him for two decades.) What about the fact that he has been deeply remorseful for years? As he wrote in one of several letters to me:

> I feel a profound sense of guilt: an intense, overwhelming, and pervasive guilt that surrounds my soul with dark, tormenting clouds of self-hatred, remorse, and sorrow… Reconciliation is what I yearn for most: reconciliation with the spirit of my victims, with their families and friends, and finally with myself and God.

It is extremely unlikely that Michael will ever be forgiven by the families of his victims. It is also as good as impossible that the courts will commute his sentence from death to life imprisonment. Still, I have tried to help him see that the fate imposed on him by the law does not have to be the last word.

No matter how tortured the state of his soul, a person like Michael, who is willing to acknowledge his guilt, is far more likely to find redemption than someone whose admission has been extracted by persuasion or threats. Even if he is denied forgiveness until the day he dies, we must hope and believe that its power can touch him – if only because he yearns for it so desperately, and because he is so determined to become worthy of it.

While it is plain that forgiveness can transform lives on a personal level, we should not forget that it can influence events on a broader scale as well. In fact, what begins as a change in one individual may affect those around him in such a way that its ripples spread wider and wider, from one person to the next.

About one hundred and fifty years ago, Möttlingen – a village in the Black Forest – experienced just such a movement. Before then, its now famous pastor, Johann Christoph Blumhardt, often sighed about the "fog of apathy" that lay over his parish. Today, aside from the streams of curious visitors that flock to see its church, the place seems equally sleepy. But a plaque on the half-timbered wall of an old house attests to remarkable events that once swept the village off its feet: "Man: think on eternity, and do not mock the time of grace, for judgment is at hand!"

The "awakening" at Möttlingen, as it is referred to today, began on New Year's Eve 1843, when a young man known for his wild carousing and violent temper came to the rectory door. After pleading to see Blumhardt, he was let in. Once inside, the man confided that he hadn't slept for a whole week, and feared that he would die if he couldn't unburden his conscience. Blumhardt, somewhat cautious, remained aloof at first, but when the man began pouring out a torrent of misdeeds, large and small, he realized the confession was an earnest one.

Thus began an unprecedented wave of confessions in which one remorseful villager after another came to reveal secret sins, and to seek the relief of starting over with a clean conscience. By January 27, 1844 sixteen people had come to the rectory. Three days later, the number had risen to thirty-five. Ten days later, it stood at more than one hundred and fifty. Soon people were pouring into the parish from neighboring villages as well.

In Möttlingen there was little of the emotionalism of most religious revivals – no exaggerated proclamations of wickedness or public avowals of repentance. What happened there was too quiet and sober for that. Pierced to the heart, people from all walks of life were suddenly able to see themselves in all their shabbiness, and felt compelled from within to break out of old ways.

Most significant, this movement went beyond words and emotions and produced concrete expressions of repentance and forgiveness. Stolen goods were returned, enemies reconciled, infidelities and crimes (including a case of infanticide) confessed, and broken marriages restored. Even the town drunks were affected, and stayed away from the tavern.

Having traveled to Möttlingen several times over the years to visit Blumhardt's descendants (my parents, both strongly influenced by his writings, named me after him) I have often asked myself whether the awakening that took place there was merely an isolated event. But I am sure that is not the case. If the forgiveness found by one repentant man could have such far-reaching effects in his day, why shouldn't we believe that it can have equal power in ours as well?

14

Not a Step, but a Journey

Forgiveness is not an occasional act.
It is a permanent attitude.

MARTIN LUTHER KING, JR.

When New York City policeman Steven McDonald stopped to question three youths in Central Park one day in 1986, he was shot and paralyzed from the neck down. Steve had been married less than a year, and his wife was two months pregnant.

Steven and his attacker, Shavod Jones, could not have been more different. Steven was white; Shavod was black. Steven came from the upper-middle class suburbs of Nassau County; Shavod from a Harlem housing project. Their brief encounter might have ended right there. But Steven wouldn't let it. Knowing that his attacker had just altered the course of both of their lives, he felt an uncanny connection to him, and began to write to him:

I was angry at him, but I was also puzzled, because I found I couldn't hate him. More often than not I felt sorry for him. I wanted him to turn his life to helping and not hurting people. I wanted him to find peace and purpose in his life. That's why I forgave him. It was a way of moving on, a way of putting the terrible accident behind me.

Shavod didn't answer Steven's letters at first, and when he finally did, the exchange fizzled out because Steven declined his request for help in getting parole. Then, in late 1995, only three days after his release from prison, Shavod was killed in a motorcycle accident. But Steven has never regretted reaching out to him.

I was a badge to that kid, a uniform representing the government. I was the system that let landlords charge rent for squalid apartments in broken-down tenements; I was the city agency that fixed up poor neighborhoods and drove the residents out, through gentrification, regardless of whether they were law-abiding solid citizens, or pushers and criminals; I was the Irish cop who showed up at a domestic dispute and left without doing anything, because no law had been broken.

To Shavod Jones, I was the enemy. He didn't see me as a person, as a man with loved ones, as a husband and father-to-be. He'd bought into all the stereotypes of his community: the police are racist, they'll turn violent, so arm yourself against them. No, I couldn't blame Jones.

Society – his family, the social agencies responsible for him, the people who'd made it impossible for his parents to be together – had failed him way before he had met me in Central Park...

Over the last several years I have met Steven many times, and spoken with him on numerous occasions. A highlight of our friendship was an appearance we made in June 1999 at an event in Belfast – I as a Protestant, and Steven as a Catholic. In a joint address delivered to members of the new government, we urged them to work for reconciliation and against revenge.

When visiting Steven in his Long Island home, I am always struck by the extent of his incapacitation. Life in a wheelchair is hard enough for an elderly person to accept, but to be plucked out of an active, fun-loving life at the age of twenty-nine is devastating. Add to that a tracheostomy to breathe through, a personal nurse to hover over you twenty-four hours a day, seven days a week – and a son you have never been able to hug, let alone play ball with – and you have Steven McDonald.

Still, I have never sensed any anger or bitterness. Steven speaks quietly, almost timidly, but his words reveal the pillar of his strength: a forgiving spirit that prevents him from wallowing in self-pity and allows him to see his confinement in a positive light. A speaker at elementary schools and high schools throughout New York, Steven has given meaning to his suffering by using it to teach others about the importance of forgiving.

> Of course, I have my ups and downs. Some days, when I am not feeling very well, I can get angry. I get depressed. There have been times when I even felt like killing myself. But I have come to realize that anger is a wasted emotion…

Though Steven's story is remarkable in many ways, it is his honesty about his ups and downs that I find most significant. Steven chose to forgive rather quickly, as did many others whose stories we have already examined. Like many of them, he says he forgave so as to be able to move on, to heal, to get on with life. But Steven also says that no matter how sincerely you decide to forgive, your decision must be reaffirmed every day. And he admits that, far from being a magical key to serenity and relief, the act of forgiving carries its own measure of anguish and pain. To borrow from Dostoevsky's oft-quoted reminder about love, forgiveness in action is a "harsh and dreadful thing" compared to forgiveness in dreams.

If Steven's story illustrates the ongoing battle that follows every decision to forgive, the next one, about an eight-year-old girl named Saira Sher, shows how that battle cannot be won without a decisive first step.

Saira was three when she was hit by a car while walking across a street in Troy, New York with her mother. Months of surgery, recuperation, and therapy followed, but she never fully recovered.

Today, despite her confinement to a wheelchair and her inability to walk or use her arms and hands (she writes by holding a pen between her teeth), Saira is a spunky third grader who has dreams of becoming lead vocalist in her own rock band and founding a home for disabled children. "I'm trapped outside, but free on the inside," she wrote in a recent issue of her school newspaper. "I probably do more than anyone else that can walk. Over all, being paralyzed isn't so bad."

But if you talk to grandmother (and primary caregiver) Alice Calonga, you'll get another angle of the picture:

> Saira's an inspiration. She doesn't have any animosity at all. She is a very positive human being, and doesn't dwell on what happened to her or feel sorry for herself. She's just a normal kid, as far as she's concerned. As much as was taken from her, she's given that much back a thousand times in her short life to the people around her. But that still doesn't undo what was done to her...
>
> I'll never forget the first couple of days after the accident. We were up in Albany in the pediatric ICU and

there were a lot of people milling around with their children. But there were two young men there who kind of stood out, because they were always there, watching me. Finally one of them approached me and asked me if I was related to the little girl who got hit by the car. I said I was. Then he asked me if I was her grandmother. I said yes.

At this point I asked him who he was, and he said he was the man who had hit her. I was stunned. Then he asked me if I could forgive him. When I tried to put myself in this stranger's shoes and think how devastated I would feel if I were him, I right away knew I had to forgive him. So I did. Then I hugged him.

Just at that moment my daughter came out of the ICU. She was horrified to see me talking with this man and was very angry at me.

She started telling me how the accident had happened – how the driver had been so impatient, he had driven around the vehicle in front of him, which had stopped for a traffic light, and run into her and Saira. Then, trying to flee the scene, he had accelerated and hit Saira a second time, breaking her neck and crushing her spine.

At first I couldn't believe it. I said, "Nobody would do anything like that." But I soon found out that my daughter was not exaggerating. I was so horrified, I felt like I had been raped. I had been robbed of my forgiveness by a man who wasn't the least bit entitled to it...

Alice says that despite her shock – and the fury of her daughter, who told her she had no right to forgive anyone for what happened – she is certain she did the right thing.

> As angry as some people are that I did it, in my heart I know I forgave that driver for the right reason, even if I was just going on instinct. I can honestly say that if I had not forgiven him at that particular moment, I might never have been able to. It's so clear to me now that he didn't deserve it. But if I were him – if I had done what he did – I know I would still want forgiveness. That's how I was thinking when I originally forgave him.
>
> Of course, since then I've found out a lot more about that driver. He's continued to flout the law and to do bodily harm to others without showing any kind of remorse. Last I heard he had thirty-seven violations on his license! When he hit Saira he already had nineteen. Lord only knows what else he has done.

Alice says it's a daily fight to hang on to her initial offer of forgiveness. But she also says that the struggle has made her a stronger person.

> It's taken me such a long time to get over the feeling of having been used. A long time. But I *have* gotten over it. I don't think he'll ever be worthy of my forgiveness. Still, I can carry my burdens a whole lot easier now, than when I had to carry my anger around as well. And be-

cause of that I can live a better life and give my energy to someone who deserves it – someone like Saira.

By illustrating the power of forgiveness in their own lives, people like Steven and Alice make exemplary models for others who want to forgive. But ultimately they are just that: models. And if their stories are to be of any real use beyond merely edifying us, we must find the points at which their journeys intersect with our own.

Obviously, the road to healing and wholeness cannot be the same for everyone. Every person moves at his or her own pace, and there are different paths to the same destination. Some people find strength to forgive within themselves, others through the help of those around them. Some are able to forgive only when they recognize their own inadequacy and turn to a higher power. Still others are never really able to forgive at all.

Terry, a local prison inmate I correspond with, is thirty-seven years old. So far he's spent nineteen of them in prisons, jails, or detention homes of one kind or another. Forcibly abducted from his abusive parents by child welfare agents determined to save him and his siblings, Terry and his brothers were shunted from one foster home to another over a period of two decades.

In one foster home Terry was severely beaten by the woman in charge; at another, repeatedly raped by older roommates. In yet another home, the priest who ran it molested him. Multiple escapes were followed by multiple recaptures, which were followed by days of solitary confinement in a locked room, his food passed through a slot in the door, and nothing to wear but undershorts.

Terry has spent so much of his life on drugs and alcohol that parts of his youth are only a blur. He has attempted suicide too many times to count. Still, he yearns to forgive the people who have made his life the hell it is, to forgive himself for the "stupid choices" he recognizes that he himself made along the way, and to be forgiven for the crimes (burglary and drunk driving) that have landed him in jail.

> I'll sit and tell you every one of my sins, and I am truly very sorry for every one, even for the ones I'm not even aware of. Believe me, I've got a good heart. I'd give whatever I have if someone asked me. I love other people but hate myself. Does that make any sense? It hurts me to see someone else hurt, but at the same time I've hurt every person I ever loved. Are all my emotions directed in the wrong places, or am I just a real screwball?
>
> To be honest, a lot of my problems have to do with holding on to grudges. I do not know how to let them go. There's so much pent-up anger in me, so much hate

and bitterness inside, I'm just not able to truly love. Nothing seems to be able to block the demons in my head or take away the unexplained pain I feel each and every day.

When I'm with other people, I can fake it. I joke around, I laugh. But once I'm alone, I get sober, and all these feelings – loneliness, abandonment, revenge, suicide – come welling up and take hold of me. I've undergone psychiatric counseling; I've been through rehab and halfway houses. I've been on every medication there is. But nothing works for me. Nothing.

I've begged Jesus to come into my life so many times, and part of him has, or I wouldn't be writing this letter to you. But how do I get rid of all the crap that takes up so much space in my mind? I feel like I'm unable to make a conscious decision to stop hating…

My childhood is over and done, I know, but I am still pissed off at my parents because of what they did to me and my brothers when we were kids. Sometimes I lie in bed at night dreaming about how I'd punch them in the face if I ever saw them again. I know the Bible says, Honor your father and mother. But I can't. I try to. I try very hard. But I just can't let my anger go. I am so messed up by my childhood. Last time I saw my oldest brother, he was dying of AIDS. Another brother has been in a mental hospital for forty years now. Another lives upstate and beats the hell out of his children, like Dad beat the hell out of him. I've called the child protection agency on him several times…

I pray for forgiveness. I pray for other people. I pray that God can help me to become the person he wants me to be. I pray that I can accept anything thrown at me in the course of a day. I pray that I can accept who I am.

I need to learn how to rid myself of the hate I feel, because it's killing me. One of my biggest fears is dying in this prison. I'm scared my soul would be stuck here.

I honestly want to forgive those I hate – including my parents – even though dark thoughts enter my mind all the time, and I have to pray daily to remove them. I see my own need for forgiveness too. I want so badly to be a good person and to change my ways.

I've read in the Bible about how Jesus touched people and transformed their lives. They only had to get close enough to him to touch his robe, and then they'd be healed. I know I'm only a speck of dust among millions of others, but I wish I could find that healing for myself. Or am I expecting too much?

Terry may never be able to confront the people who need his forgiveness, or come to terms with the suffering he has endured at their hands. Even if he did, he might never be able to pull himself together and verbalize the forgiveness he wishes he could grant them. In a situation like his, where the fear of being misunderstood or trampled on is very great, it may be too painful to expose one's deepest feelings.

In the end, however, it is not words that matter. For Terry, as for each of us, it is our inmost attitude that really counts. That is what will tip the scales of our lives in the direction we really want to go, no matter how many conflicting emotions threaten to throw us off balance.

When Bud Welch lost his 23-year-old daughter Julie, he lost the pride of his life, and to this day he cannot say he has forgiven the man who killed her. Still, he refuses to give resentment and despair the upper hand, and tries instead to keep her memory alive by sharing his pride in her with others.

> I'm the third of eight children and grew up on a dairy farm, and I've run a service station in Oklahoma City for the last thirty-four years. Until April 19, 1995 – the day Julie and 167 others were killed in the bomb blast that destroyed the Alfred P. Murrah Building – my life was very simple. I had a little girl and loved her a lot.
>
> Julie had a rough start; she was born premature, but she survived and grew healthy and strong. She had just graduated from Marquette with a degree in Spanish and started a job as a translator for the Social Security Administration. At the time of her death she was dating an Air Force lieutenant named Eric. The day after Julie was killed I found out that they had decided to announce their engagement in two weeks.

All my life I have opposed the death penalty. Friends used to tell me that if anyone ever killed one of my family members, I would change. "What if Julie got raped and murdered?" But I always said I'd stick to my guns. Until April 19.

The first four or five weeks after the bombing I had so much anger, pain, hatred, and revenge, that I realized why, when someone is charged with a violent crime, they transport him in a bullet-proof vest. It's because people like me would try to kill him.

By the end of 1995 I was in such bad shape, I was drinking heavily and smoking three packs of cigarettes a day. I was stuck, emotionally, on April 19. I just couldn't get over it. But I knew I had to do something about it. That's when I went down to the bombing site.

It was a cold January afternoon, and I stood there watching hundreds of people walking along the chain link fence that surrounded the lot where the Murrah Building had stood. I was thinking about the death penalty, and how I wanted nothing more than to see Timothy McVeigh (and anyone else responsible for the bombing) fried. But I was also beginning to wonder whether I would really feel any better once they were executed. Every time I asked myself that question, I got the same answer: No. Nothing positive would come from it. It wouldn't bring Julie back. After all, it was hatred and revenge that made me want to see them dead, and those two things were the very reason that Julie and 167 others were dead...

Once he arrived at this realization, Bud returned to his original belief that executing criminals was wrong, and he has since become a leading opponent of the death penalty. Sought across the country as a speaker on the futility of capital punishment, he makes appearances in churches and town meetings, on college campuses and at activist gatherings. He is always on the go. But nothing he has done means as much to him as his meeting with Timothy's father:

> A person like Bill McVeigh is as much a victim as I am, if not more. I can't imagine the pain he and his family have been through. I've lost a daughter, and if Timothy is ever executed he's going to lose a son. I have a son myself, and if he was convicted of killing 168 people, I don't know how I'd deal with that. Bill has to live with that for the rest of his life.
>
> I first saw Bill McVeigh on television a few weeks after the bombing. He was working in his flower bed, and he looked up at the camera for a couple seconds. When he did I saw a father with deep, deep pain in his eyes. I could recognize it, because I was living that pain. I knew right then that someday I had to go tell him that I truly cared how he felt.
>
> So I did. The day I visited him he was out in his garden again, and we spent about half an hour just getting acquainted, kicking dirt and pulling weeds. Then we went into the house so I could meet Jennifer, his 24-year-

old daughter. As we walked in I noticed a few family photos on the wall over the kitchen table. The largest one was of Timothy. I kept glancing up at that picture. I knew that they were watching me, so I said, "Gosh, what a good-looking kid." Bill had told me outdoors that he was having a lot of trouble showing emotion – that he couldn't cry. But when I commented on that photograph he said, "That's Tim's high school graduation picture," and a great big tear rolled down his cheek.

We talked for another hour and a half. When I got ready to leave I shook Bill's hand and extended my hand to Jennifer. She didn't take it. She hugged me around the neck. I don't know who started crying first as we embraced, but we were both in tears. Finally I said, "Honey, we're in this together for the rest of our lives. And we can make the most of it, if we choose. I don't want your brother to die, and I'll do everything in my power to prevent it." Never in my life have I felt closer to God than I did at that time. I felt like a thousand pounds had been lifted off my shoulders.

Still, Bud says he has no desire to meet his daughter's killer. Sometimes he's not even sure he's really forgiven him:

> ...At least I don't think I have forgiven him. I was speaking at Oklahoma State University one time, and the Bishop of Tulsa was there. I was telling the group about my struggle, and that I didn't feel that I had forgiven him. Anyway, the bishop chimed in and said, "But I think you *have* forgiven him." And he started quoting some verse

from Scripture, which I'm not very good at doing. But he's a bishop, and I suppose he's qualified. I guess he was trying to convince me that I have forgiven Timothy, and maybe I have.

I still have my moments of rage. I remember crossing the campus of a high school in California, on my way to speak to an all-school assembly, and looking around as I walked. The place reminded me of Julie's high school. Suddenly this rage just hit me. So here I was, getting ready to speak to a whole auditorium full of kids about my opposition to the death penalty, and I was thinking to myself, "That bastard doesn't even deserve to live."

I know I don't want Timothy executed, because once he's gone, it will be to late to choose to forgive him. As long as he's alive, I have to deal with my feelings and emotions. But I do have setbacks, even when I'm sure I want to forgive. That's probably why I can't handle that word "closure." I get sick of hearing it. The first time someone asked me about closure was the day after Julie's burial. Of course I was still in hell then. In a way, I still am. How can there ever be true closure? A part of my heart is gone.

Bud has been an inspiration to me from the very first time we met, and each time I see him, I sense an increased determination to make the best he can of the tragedy that hit him. While it was grief that first led him to visit the family of his daughter's killer, it is her life-affirming spirit that drives him now. And even if he hasn't yet found the full measure of healing he seeks, his journey – like every journey of forgiveness – is one of hope:

It's a struggle, but it's one I need to wage. In any case, forgiving is not something you just wake up one morning and decide to do. You have to work through your anger and your hatred as long as it's there. You try to live each day a little better than the one before.

EPILOGUE

At the beginning of this book I wrote about a man who had murdered a seven-year-old girl. I asked, Can such a man be forgiven? In the years since I first met him, this man has undergone a remarkable change. Whereas at first he was emotionally numb and tended to see his crime as the inevitable result of society's ills, he has now begun to accept responsibility for his own actions. And he has begun to agonize over his need for forgiveness – to weep for others, rather than for himself. In meeting this man, I have seen forgiveness as it begins to work in someone who confronts the gravity of his deeds, admits his guilt, and recognizes the necessity of remorse.

Can such a man be forgiven? If we truly believe in the transforming power of forgiveness, we must believe that he can. Of course we must never belittle his capacity for violence or condone the evil of his crime. But neither can we condemn him as hopeless and deny him the opportunity to change. No matter how repeatedly we ourselves demonstrate the same shortcomings, we still want others to forgive us, and to believe that we can change. As Jesus of Nazareth put it so many centuries ago, "Let him who is without sin cast the first stone."

Forgiveness is power. It frees us from every constraint of the past, and helps us overcome every obstacle. It can heal both the forgiver and the forgiven. In fact, it could change the world if we allowed it to. But too often we stand in its way, not daring to let it flow through us unchecked. In short, we hold the keys to forgiveness in our hands. And we must choose whether or not to use them every day.

INDEX OF NAMES

THE AUTHOR

People have come to expect good reading from Johann Christoph Arnold, whose books have sold over 350,000 copies in English and have been translated into nineteen other languages.

Arnold brings an uncommon wealth of experience and depth of insight to his writing. For decades he and his wife, Verena, have counseled hundreds of individuals and couples, including prison inmates, teenagers, and the terminally ill. He is a frequent guest on talk shows and a popular speaker at schools and conferences.

An outspoken social critic, Arnold advocates a consistent reverence for life and has participated in peace initiatives around the world. Recent journeys have taken him to Northern Ireland, the Middle East, and Central America — and into schools, hospitals, refugee camps, and prisons.